Praise for *Tell Me...*
And Fred Reggie

Not only will *Tell Me...* provide you with timeless wisdom bombs in mastering your storytelling IQ, but you will also get the real life, from-the-street secrets that make conversations truly meaningful. Isn't that what you need in your effort to become *significant* and *influential?*
–MARVIN LEBLANC, LUTCF, CNP, author of *Come Hell or High Water: Life Lessons from Hurricane Katrina*

Tell Me... is a masterclass in the lost art of meaningful conversation. Fred Reggie delivers a practical, engaging, and deeply human guide to connecting with anyone–anytime, anywhere. Whether you want to strengthen relationships, lead with impact, or simply never struggle with small talk again, this book hands you the keys. Read it. Use it. Watch your world transform–one conversation at a time.
–DAVID NEWMAN, author of *Do It! Marketing* and *Do It! Selling*

The development I have personally seen over the last year has truly transformed how I navigate interactions with partners and customers. The phrase "Tell Me..." is empowering because it truly allows one to gain total buy-in while creating a sense of ownership for both parties within the conversation.
–WESLEY STIGLETS, branch manager of Cintas Corporation

Tell Me... is a great and valuable take on the most misunderstood human medium of verbal exchange. There is a difference between talk and conversation–between words and connection. Fred Reggie shows us how to convey who we really are and capitalize on our gifts and talents to be more communicative–more intentional–much clearer on how we exchange ideas.
–DARRELL PALOMBO, CEO of Crescent Search, Inc.

I truly enjoyed Fred Reggie's new book, *Tell Me... How to Initiate and Nurture Meaningful Conversations with Anyone, Anywhere, Anytime.* Everyone can find something useful in this gem of a book. Fred's writing style is engaging, and his straightforward skills-building practices will transform your way of thinking about how to interact with people in a truly authentic way. Some highlights include practical tips from his P-A-I-L-E-R Method, thoughtful insights about how critical body language is, and how the art of listening is so important in genuine human connections, among so many other highlights. I highly recommend this common sense book, packed with wisdom and helpful ideas.

—MICHAEL J. LYONS, published author, professional speaker, SAG-AFTRA actor, entrepreneur

Fred Reggie's TMT (*Tell Me* Technique) is an invaluable tool I use to train and equip teachers as well as when I teach students of all ages. His ability to dissect a communication obstacle and then provide a pathway forward to overcome it is both insightful and encouraging. Reggie targets the heart of the matter and scores a bullseye! Well done.

—AL ZWAN, Christian educator

In nearly twenty years of working in B2B marketing, I've learned one lesson time and time again—companies do business with PEOPLE, not companies. And being able to truly connect via conversation is at the root of it all. *Tell Me...* invites you to master this age-old gift of conversation. Be sure this is one invitation you accept!

—JON FRANKO, co-founder of Gorilla 76

Ever dreaded going to a party, afraid you won't know what to say? Or feared engaging in a work setting, feeling unsure you can competently participate in the conversation? Do not despair. After reading *Tell Me... How to Initiate and Nurture Meaningful Conversations with*

Anyone, Anywhere, Anytime by author and renowned executive coach Fred Reggie, your fears will be alleviated. *Tell Me...* thoroughly and expertly defines and analyzes the art and science of conversation. Reggie explains with great insight that meaningful communication is the bedrock of a meaningful life. His book leaves no stone unturned in giving the reader every fact and aid needed to conquer fears and become fully engaged in the world at hand.
—TESSIE PATTERSON, retired publicist

A thoroughly enjoyable read. *Tell Me...* focuses on practical advice for building genuine human connection through meaningful conversation and storytelling. A must-read resource to elevate everyday dialogue.
—NANCY BROADHURST, associate vice president and executive director of Ochsner Lafayette General Foundation

What an amazing book! I was once a shy person who often struggled with conversations, unsure how to start or keep them flowing. Reading *Tell Me...* made me realize how a simple shift—inviting others in with "Tell Me..."—could have transformed my interactions, from meeting new people to connecting more deeply with clients or my children. This book has given me invaluable tools to foster meaningful conversations with confidence and ease.
—YVONNE BALENTINE, estimating coordinator for Shreve Land Construction, LLC

A must-read for anyone looking to communicate with confidence! *Tell Me...* is a game-changer for those who struggle with conversation. With its simple yet powerful techniques, this book makes it easy to start engaging discussions and build meaningful connections. It is packed with practical strategies for overcoming communication barriers, fostering trust, and making a lasting impact in both personal and professional settings. Whether you're looking to navigate difficult

conversations or simply become a more confident communicator, this book is an invaluable resource. Absolute best read in a long while!
—J. TYLER GILMAN, Group One Sotheby's International Realty

Anyone in management, or who aspires to be, should read this book. After suffering stage fright many years, I learned from it how much more relaxed and effective I could have been in my lengthy career as a government administrator.
—ANN DAVENPORT, retired government administrator for the State of Louisiana

Fred Reggie is a master of meaningful conversations. I've learned so much from listening to what he has to say. I wish I would have learned these lessons years ago! I've been passing his wisdom on to my grandchildren, and it's heartwarming to witness the impact. *Tell Me...* is a must-read!
—DAN DIAMOND, MD, author of *Beyond Resilience*

In a world of texts, DMs, and endless scrolling, *Tell Me...* shows how two simple words can spark real conversations, deepen connections, and bring meaning back to the way we communicate.
—JEFF PUGEL, founder & CEO of Ignition, LLC

Working in the addiction field, I am always looking for ways to effectively communicate with my clients. The simplicity of the book, *Tell Me...* was most helpful in teaching me to genuinely communicate and connect with not only clients, but family members as well.
—TOOTIE LANDRY, registered addiction counselor and national interventionist

Every once in a while, a book comes along that changes the way we connect with others. 'Tell Me...' is that book. It belongs right next to 'How to Win Friends and Influence People' on your bookshelf as a timeless reference to building meaningful relationships through the

power of conversation. With masterful storytelling and actionable insights, Fred Reggie shows us that two simple words—'Tell Me'—can open doors, foster trust, and transform the way we engage with the world.
—LYNN DUNSTAN, retired educator and congressional liaison

Fred Reggie's *Tell Me...* is a powerful reminder that conversations are not just about exchanging words—they are about opening doors to deeper understanding. His simple yet profound "Tell Me..." approach beautifully aligns with my own work on the power of pausing to foster connection. This book reinforces that when we slow down, get curious, and truly listen, we create space for conversations that move beyond the transactional into the transformational. In a world of quick exchanges, *Tell Me...* is an invitation to reimagine how we engage with one another.
—MO (MAUREEN) MCKENNA, eclectic explorer, Return on Energy

As a therapist who uses conversation as a primary tool to engage and help my clients, I couldn't be happier for the release of *Tell Me...* In my work I see the effect that the shift toward digital interaction has had on the art of having a conversation. More and more I hear clients using words like *awkward*, *frustrating*, and *demoralizing* to describe their experience having in-person interactions. I see firsthand the anxiety and stress that many experience when thinking about the possibility of having to strike up a conversation. This book, this toolbox, compiled from Fred's decades of conversations with people from every walk of life, will help anyone improve their ability to converse and more importantly increase their confidence.
—ROY PETITFILS, psychotherapist-counselor, author of *Helping Teens with Stress, Anxiety, and Depression*

Effective communication skills are a must-have, in both business and life. *Tell Me...* is a must-have for developing your communication skills. I love how Fred synthesized decades of mastery into a simple, practical book. The "Pause and Ponder" moments truly helped me absorb the lessons along the way.

—JEFF MARTIN, author of the #1 bestselling book *Business Mulligan: How to Give Your Business and Your Life a Second Chance in a Changing World*

Outstanding! Two chapters that really stood out to me were the one on storytelling and 'becoming the story' and the one offering insight on how 'Tell Me' compels real listening and engagement. Incredibly powerful. Most people don't fully grasp just how transformative storytelling and listening can be, but this book makes it crystal clear. I'll be picking up multiple copies to share.

—GEORGES ANTOUN, chief commercial officer of First Solar

In *Tell Me... How to Initiate and Nurture Meaningful Conversations with Anyone, Anywhere, Anytime*, Fred Reggie masterfully lays out a practice which enhances communication and connection in a world where both are lacking. This book shows you how to navigate every conversation with confidence and clarity through practical examples, real-world scenarios, and insights from the latest communication studies. More than just techniques, it emphasizes the importance of character, compassion, and empathy, offering tools to build deeper relationships, foster trust, and create meaningful impact. Whether engaging in personal discussions or professional negotiations, this book equips you with the skills to communicate authentically and kindly. It speaks to the essence of Fred, who believes in adding value to every person he meets. *Tell Me...* has opened and improved my effectiveness in relationships and as a presenter.

—MIKE PATIN, Catholic speaker, consultant, and author of *This Was Not in the Brochure: Lessons from Work, Ministry, and Life*

Fred Reggie's *Tell Me...* nails it on so many levels. He brings us all up to date on the age-old art of conversation every leader needs to master, and with wit and humor to boot. Having coached Fortune 500 execs to own any room, virtual and real, I was hooked from the Table of Contents alone. Reggie dishes out a smorgasbord of skills—storytelling, vocal flair, eye gaze, subtle non-verbal cues that pull us in. It's the perfect companion for a workforce tangled in hybrid chaos, young employees raised on screens, and older generations who fight the urge to reach for our phones. This is a fresh, practical playbook, mixing simple gems with sharp techniques, sticky stories, and numerous ah-ha moments that deliver with impact.

—CINDY SKALICKY, founder of On Point Communications and author of *Red Light, Green Light: How Top Leaders Present with Polish, Get Buy-in, and Become More Influential*

Tell Me... is a masterclass in impactful communication, transforming a simple phrase into a powerful framework for authentic connection. Fred Reggie seamlessly blends practical strategies—from body language and active listening to question frameworks and engagement techniques—making complex concepts both accessible and immediately actionable. While leaders will find valuable insights on fostering psychological safety within teams, the book's principles benefit anyone seeking deeper, more meaningful relationships. By applying these techniques, individuals can make others feel genuinely valued while advancing shared goals. For those who believe strong relationships are the key to success, this book is not just recommended—it's essential.

—RUSTY GAILLARD, leadership development coach and former worldwide director of finance at Apple, author of *Breaking the Code*

A masterful manual on how to action emotional intelligence fundamentals with practical applications and genuine curiosity.

—ELEONORA M. MIGLIACCIO, ESQ., global law senior client relationship partner

There's always a magical feeling that comes over us when we find ourselves connecting with others in deep, meaningful, and authentic conversations. We can feel the excitement, joy, and energy building as these powerful conversations connect us, build bridges, and transform our relationships. Fred Reggie has done just that. His new book, *Tell Me...*, is beautifully written, well-crafted, and deeply moving. Using heartfelt stories, powerful examples, and pause-and-ponder moments, the book takes the reader on a journey through the art and science of creating powerful conversations. Reggie writes from the heart and speaks to your heart as he shares his insights on how to connect with any audience for any purpose. Whether you are looking to grow in your familial, social, or professional communication skills, *Tell Me...* is sure to grow your confidence, transform your life, and elevate your conversations. This is a book for everyone! I cannot wait to fill my classroom and school library with it!
—KATHY DURHAM, educator at West Wendover High School, Wendover, Nevada

Let me tell you that you need to read *Tell Me...* if you want to connect rather than converse. I've taught communication skills to over 200,000 people and *Tell Me...* is practical. While it is essential for people new to their careers, I kept coming across things that would help me. When I speak regarding generational differences, I hear from people who have grown up writing on their phones that they feel nervous or awkward speaking on the phone or in person. From now on I will tell them that *this* is the help that they're looking for.
—HAYDN SHAW, author of *Sticking Points: How to Get Five Generations Working Together in the Twelve Places They Come Apart*

In a world where true connection is often lost in the noise, this book is a game-changer. The simple yet powerful *Tell Me...* technique transforms the way we communicate—breaking down organizational silos, fostering deeper conversations, and creating space for real understanding. Whether in the workplace or personal relationships, this approach is a must-have tool for anyone looking to move beyond surface-level dialogue and build stronger, more meaningful connections. You are speaking my love language, Fred, great work!

—KIKI ORSKI, MBA, RN, author of *Smash the Silos!: A Surprisingly Easy Way to Enhance Collaboration, Boost Productivity, and Improve Organizational Results*

Tell Me... is both literary and heart-enlarging—a book you can read purely for pleasure or for practical learning. Fred masterfully shows readers how to encourage family, friends, and colleagues by engaging in conversations that are both comfortable and revealing. Packed with vivid anecdotes, insightful guidance, and compelling data, this book is essential reading for anyone seeking to understand the power of listening and making others feel heard. So, *Tell Me...*

—MARY BETH ISTRE, retired educator

I wish I had had this resource when I was engaged in my forty-four-year banking career. "Tell Me" would have been the first tool I would have employed when meeting with clients and colleagues. What a difference it would have made in my goal of making meaningful connections with them. But all is not lost. I will now use what I learned from *Tell Me...* to deepen my relationships with my family and friends. Thank you, Fred Reggie, for sharing your insights and experiences in such a well-written and relatable book.

—RICHARD FRUGÉ, retired private banking officer

As an enthusiastically unapologetic extrovert, few things make me happier than engaging with other people and learning about their stories. After reading this book, I'm looking forward to employing techniques like "Tell Me..." and the PAILER Method to start new conversations in my own day to day interactions. I can't think of a better

book for someone who might be trying to figure out how to break out of their own shell and start connecting with others. Fred Reggie has truly cooked up something special with this one.
—CREIGHTON SHUTE, DO, Elite DPC

Tell Me... is the perfect book at the perfect time! It's a treasure trove of information about having meaningful conversations with those we love, as well as strangers. The most important and powerful of Reggie's "how-tos" is making each person feel that they are the most important person in the room; something he does in every conversation. I have tried his techniques with both family and strangers and have been having much more meaningful encounters.
—FAY BOWEN, retired journalist

The beauty of *Tell Me...* is that it applies to communication whether in sales, the corporate board room, or within family. I will buy this book for both of my daughters and one each for my four grandchildren for use as a family study. I believe studying "Tell Me..." as a family will greatly improve the family dynamic while teaching my grandchildren the art of effective communication that will serve them well in life. I am confident that it will do wonders for their self-confidence and mental health. My sister was a victim of the current over-stimulated and over-medicated world that has been cast upon us resulting in her suicide. Implementing *Tell Me...* as a family book-study will help prevent family tragedies as we experienced.
—NEAL HEBERT, CFP, financial advisor at Gulf Coast Bank

In my 35 years in high-end jewelry sales, I've learned that building relationships is the key to success. Fred Reggie's *Tell Me...* is right on the mark—engaging people in conversation makes them feel valued and at ease, transforming transactions into lasting connections. This approach has been the foundation of my success, leading to loyal

clients and repeat business. If you want to master the art of meaningful conversations, this book is your key!
—DEBORAH REBSTOCK, sales executive, Deutsch & Deutsch Jewelers

Tell Me... is a powerful tool for building relationships and driving success in commercial construction. Fred Reggie's approach enhances client conversations by uncovering key insights that strengthen sales and negotiations. By applying these principles, I've seen firsthand how trust and engagement lead to better deals and long-term partnerships.
—KATIE MULRENIN, director of business development, International Contractors, Inc.

In "Tell Me" Fred Reggie outlines a simple approach to engaging others in conversation under just about any imaginable circumstance. Get them talking with the phrase "tell me... ." Grounded in empathy, this advice gives both conversational partners a role to play. Aptly, the various chapters come alive with vignettes that prove the power of stories to inform us and make genuine connections. Put down your phone and start listening!
—PATRICIA O'CONNELL, content strategist and co-author of *"Woo, Wow, and Win: Service Design, Strategy, and the Art of Customer Delight*

Technology has made communication faster and more convenient—but at a cost. As we rely more on digital interactions, our ability to truly connect with people weakens. Fred Reggie's "Tell Me..." is the antidote. He offers a practical roadmap to strengthening our people-connection muscle, providing actionable tips to immediately improve our interactions. His engaging anecdotes make these lessons unforgettable. You may forget the advice—but you'll always remember the stories that bring it to life.
—CAPIZ GREENE, president and owner of Greenelight Professional Development

Fred Reggie hit this one out of the park. *Tell Me...* is a step-by-step guide to showing up in the moment. It is an invitation to arrive at the pinnacle of human connection together, to learn how to hold space for the experiences of another and to truly learn once and for all, how to listen. If you want to learn how to communicate on a whole new level, this is the book that will get you there.
—JEN CRONEBERGER, founder of Human Leadership Institute, four-time TEDx speaker, and published author.

In *Tell Me . . .* , Fred Reggie captures the essence of genuine connection through the power of two simple words. As a leadership coach specializing in strategic planning, I see firsthand how the most successful planning sessions thrive on open dialogue, collaboration, and engagement. The practical takeaways in this book provide a game-changing approach to fostering deeper conversations that lead to more innovative ideas and better alignment. Whether you're leading a team, facilitating a strategic planning session, or simply aiming to connect more meaningfully, *Tell Me . . .* is an invaluable resource.
—RITA BARRETO, president of Top Tier Leadership

Tell Me is an invitation to make a meaningful connection - a key component in a successful teaching and learning relationship and classroom environment. It is a must read (and put into practice!) for both teachers and their students as a way to maximize engagement and foster relationships in and outside of the classroom.
—JEANNE FRUGÉ-RODRIGUEZ, PhD, educator

Fred Reggie offers readers a straightforward, common-sense approach to sparking meaningful conversations in any professional or personal setting. By simply using the two powerful words, "Tell me," he shows how to engage others through their experiences, history, personal stories, or professional insights. This book is a must-read for anyone looking to build confidence and strengthen interpersonal skills.

—JIM WELLS, senior vice president of UrbanStreet Group, LLC

#1 BEST SELLER

How to **Initiate** and **Nurture**
MEANINGFUL CONVERSATIONS
with **Anyone, Anywhere, Anytime**

FRED REGGIE

Ajibi
PUBLISHING

Tell Me . . .
How to Initiate and Nurture
MEANINGFUL CONVERSATIONS
with Anyone, Anywhere, Anytime

Copyright © 2025 Fred Reggie. All rights reserved. Printed in the United States of America.

The ideas, stories, and strategies shared in this book are intended to inform, encourage, and inspire more meaningful conversations. They are based on the author's personal experiences, observations, and research. While every effort has been made to ensure accuracy and relevance, every reader's circumstances are unique. The author and publisher make no guarantees regarding specific outcomes and recommend that readers exercise their own judgment in applying the material.

This book is not a substitute for professional advice when needed. The author and publisher disclaim any liability for any loss or consequence arising from the application of the information provided. Above all, readers are encouraged to approach every conversation with curiosity, authenticity, and an open heart.

No part of this book may be reproduced, distributed, or transmitted in any form or by any means, including photocopying, recording, or other electronic or mechanical methods, without the prior written permission of the publisher or author.

Editor: Deborah King

ISBN 979-8-218-67654-4

To
Pookie, Jolie, Missy, Joe, Ella, and Emilio

And to
Aunt Doris

Table of Contents

Introduction	1
Why You Bought This Book	1
What's Inside	3
Final Thought	5
1 Why I Wrote This Book	7

Part 1 : Why Conversation Is So Hard 11

2 The Conversation Crisis	13
Why Are Conversations So Hard?	14
You Won't Be Remembered for Your Texts	15
The Decline of Face-to-Face Communication in the Workplace	15
Why Push Through the Discomfort?	16
The Breakthrough: Choosing Conversation over Convenience	16
3 Don't Break The Rules	21
Out of the Cradle and into the Spotlight	21
All Shut-*tered* Up	23
4 The Conversational Cocoon	29
The Automobile: A Case Study in Isolation	29
Radio and TV: The Siren Song of the Living Room	30
The Digital Age: Connected Yet Cocooned	31
The Great Irony	32
Glimmer of Hope	33
From Smartphone Cocoon to Conversational Butterfly	33

A New Dialogue	35
5 The Power of "Tell Me . . ."	**39**
Unlocking Connection in Every Conversation	39
Why "Tell Me . . ." Matters	40
Mastering the Art of "Tell Me . . ."	41
Change the Flow of Conversation	43
What Makes "Tell Me . . ." Unique and Significant?	44
Transactional to Transformational	45
Beyond Words	47

Part 2 : Take The Leap 49

6 Digging Deeper	**51**
Emma's Epiphany	52
It's Your Turn	54
7 Overcoming Impostor Syndrome	**59**
The Power of Self-Doubt	60
Missed Opportunities	61
Breaking the Cycle	62
The Value of Connection	63
8 The P-A-I-L-E-R Method	**67**
The P-A-I-L-E-R Method in Action	71

Part 3 : The Science Factor 75

9 The Neuroscience of Conversation	**77**
Why Talking Is Good for Your Brain (and Your Soul)	77
The Need for Social Interaction	77
The Brain: Your Ultimate Conversation Partner	78

What Happens to Your Brain During a Conversation	79
The EQ Boost: How Conversations Make You Smarter	80
Conversations Keep Your Brain Sharp	81
The Bigger Picture	82
10 What Your Body Says	**85**
The Power of a Genuine Smile	86
Eye Contact: A Gateway to Connection	86
Posture: Communicating Openness and Presence	86
Gestures	87
The Role of Relaxation in Conversation	87
Upspeak, Vocal Fry, and Filler Words: Their Impact on Credibility	88
Creating an Inviting Environment	91
The Takeaway: Be Genuine to Build Connection	92
11 The Subtle Art of Listening	**95**
Active Listening	95
Why Listening Is Harder Than You Think	96
The Anatomy of Active Listening	97
The Listener's Commitment	99
The Impact of Active Listening	100
Sophia's Dilemma	100
Listening as a Superpower	102
12 Listening Between The Lines	**105**
What Isn't Said	105
The Power of Voice Inflection	105
The Unspoken Cues of Body Language	107
The Executive's Story: A High-Stakes Decision Based on Non-Verbal Cues	108

The Weight of Silence	110
Listening for Emotion	110
Crafting Your Responses Based on What's Unsaid	111
Reading Between the Lines: The Listener's Superpower	112
13 The Power of Observation	**115**
Noticing Little Things Sparks Great Conversations	115
Why Observation Matters	115
Starting with What You See	116
The Magic of Personal Details	117
How to Sharpen Your Observational Skills	118
Why This Works: The Psychology of Being Seen	119
Conversations Born from Curiosity	120
Observation in Action	120
Observation, Conversation, and Serendipity	121
14 The Value of Showing Interest In Others	**127**
The Psychology Behind Feeling Valued	128
The Power of Asking Questions	128
An Unexpected Friendship: How Showing Interest Can Open Doors	129
Listening with Purpose	130
The Ripple Effect of Genuine Interest	131
The Empathy Connection	132
The Long-Term Impact	132
The Simple Power of Showing Interest	133

Part 4 : Putting It All To Work 137

15 Storytelling	139

The Stories Within You	139
Personal Reflection	140
The Universal Thread: How Stories Connect Us All	141
Thoughtful Use of Humor in Storytelling	143
Impact of Imagination	144
Guilty or Not Guilty	144
Memorable and Repeatable	145
Memorable and Repeatable in Seven Words	146
The Story Closed the Deal	147
16 Time Kills Deals	**151**
The Nature of Time	152
The Power of Swift Action	153
Ghosting: The Silent Deal Killer	153
The Simple Act of Picking Up the Phone	154
The Cost of Hesitation	155
17 Interviews: A Win-Win Approach	**159**
18 Tell Me About Accountability	**167**
The Problem with Accountability	168
Sarah's Story	168
Apply the "Tell Me . . ." Principle	170
The Accountability Disconnect	171
Be Comfortable Making Them Uncomfortable	171
Building a Culture of Accountability	173
19 Silos Are for Grains, not Brains	**177**
Breaking Down the Silos	177
The Story of Mark and Lisa	177
"Tell Me . . ." Changes Things	179

Building a Collaborative Culture	179
A Ripple Effect	180
20 Ripple, Resonate, Reshape	**185**
The Unseen Ripples of Our Words	185
Conversations That Change Worlds	186
The Myth of Neutrality	187
Your Words, Your World	188
No Conversation Stands Alone	188
The Responsibility of Engagement	189
The Beginning of the Beginning	**191**
Your New Story Begins	191
Acknowledgments	**193**
Notes	**197**
A Library of Conversations	**199**
About The Author	**201**

*con-ver-sa-tion *(noun)*

Kän-vər-sā-shən

a) talk between two or more people in which thoughts, feelings, and ideas are expressed, questions are asked and answered, or news and information is exchanged:
- ⇒ **have a conversation with**
- ⇒ She had a strange conversation with the man who moved in upstairs.
- ⇒ **hold/carry on a conversation**
  It's impossible to hold/carry on a conversation with all this noise going on!
- ⇒ **strike up a conversation**
  I struck up (= started) an interesting conversation with your uncle.
- ⇒ **run out of conversation**
  Whenever I'm in a social situation with my boss, we seem to run out of conversation (= things to say to each other) after two minutes![1]

"Taking a new step, uttering a new word, is what people fear most."

—*Fyodor Dostoevsky*
Crime and Punishment

Introduction

We've all been there. Standing at the edge of a conversation, feeling the weight of apprehension as we wonder how to begin. The awkward silence, the fear of saying the wrong thing, and the overwhelming pressure to make a good impression can keep us stuck in our own heads. Whether it's at a networking event, a family gathering, or a professional meeting, the challenge is the same—how do you confidently initiate a meaningful conversation?

What if there was a way to easily break through that anxiety, a method that not only helped you start a conversation but also made you feel more confident in every interaction? What if you could easily open the door to connection and opportunity?

Why You Bought This Book

So, let's talk about why you picked up this book—whether you realized it or not. Have you ever been in one of those meetings where you nail the presentation? You have your revenue numbers, KPIs, and forecasts locked in, and the room is engaged. Everything goes perfectly.

But then, the meeting ends, and everyone gathers for a reception or dinner. The "business talk" disappears, and suddenly, it's all about small talk. People are chatting about families, travel, hobbies—those human, everyday things. And there you are, thinking, *What do I even say to the CEO? Do we have anything in common? Does she care about what I have to say?*

Tell Me . . .

Here's the good news: You're not alone in feeling this way. Over the last twenty years, I have worked with clients who've admitted how uncomfortable and awkward it feels to strike up casual but meaningful conversations—especially with the people who hold the keys to their future in the company.

That's where this book, *Tell Me . . .*, comes in. It's about more than just business presentations and meetings. It's about helping you confidently step into any conversation, whether it's at a corporate event, a wedding, a gala, or even just sitting next to a stranger on a plane. It's about finding your voice in those moments when you'd usually feel stuck.

"Tell Me . . ." is also a most valuable tool to use in interviews and feedback sessions—both as the interviewer and the interviewee—as discussed in chapter 17. And let's not forget family settings—imagine finally getting your teenager (or parent!) to open up with more than just a one-word answer. This book offers practical tools to help you start and sustain meaningful conversations, no matter the situation. Reading this book will allow you to step into any conversational space with confidence and comfort. Never again will you be at a loss to initiate a conversation with anyone, anywhere, anytime.

You likely bought this book because you want to:

⇒ **Build Confidence in Your Ability to Engage in Conversation**
Many people struggle with starting conversations, but this book introduces a simple, effective approach to opening dialogue. This technique reduces apprehension, making it easier to engage with anyone in any setting.

⇒ **Foster Genuine Connections in a Distracted World**
Readers will learn how to move beyond surface-level exchanges by asking meaningful questions and actively listening—turning casual conversations into opportunities for authentic connection, trust, and understanding.

⇒ **Address Communication Barriers Head-On**
This book provides actionable tools for handling difficult or awkward conversations with clarity and empathy. Whether it's bridging generational gaps or managing workplace conflicts, *Tell Me...* offers practical solutions for creating mutual respect and accountability.

⇒ **Enhance Professional and Personal Impact**
By mastering conversational techniques rooted in curiosity and storytelling, readers can leave a lasting impression in interviews, meetings, or social settings. This book illustrates how meaningful conversations can drive success in relationships, leadership, and even sales.

⇒ **Find Common Ground Anytime, Anywhere**
Using the methods in *Tell Me...*, readers will gain the skills to connect with people of any background or personality type. From breaking the ice with strangers to deepening bonds with loved ones, this book provides a framework for building rapport and trust effortlessly.

What's Inside

Part 1: Why Conversation Is So Hard explores why starting conversations can feel intimidating for many. We'll uncover how factors like childhood conditioning, technology, and even well-meaning influences from those around us have unintentionally eroded our confidence in face-to-face interactions.

Part 2: Take the Leap prepares the reader for taking the first step into the world of conversation. It inspires the reader to be confident and provides a systematic method for initiating a conversation.

Part 3: The Science Factor delves into the physiology and psychology surrounding conversation. It explores the subtle elements that enrich conversation beyond just words. We'll discuss the roles of listening, deliberate silence, pauses, body language, and observation in creating an environment for meaningful dialogue. This section also highlights how conversations engage emotional intelligence, drawing on qualities like empathy, warmth, and compassion—human traits that no algorithm or AI can replicate.

Part 4: Putting It All to Work focuses on the practical application of the principles introduced throughout this book, ensuring these tools can be seamlessly integrated into your daily life.

It should be noted that this book goes beyond the promise of the subtitle: *How to Initiate and Nurture Meaningful Conversations with Anyone, Anywhere, Anytime.* You will also understand and appreciate how lives are changed in the process as you continually refine your ability to engage with others in significant and profound ways.

Throughout this book, you'll find **Pause and Ponder** breaks—moments where you're encouraged to briefly pause, reflect, and relate the chapter's ideas to your own experiences. These opportunities will reinforce the key messages and help you develop a conversational mindset that enhances all your future interactions. If you are listening to the audiobook, you might want to bookmark them.

At the end of each chapter, you'll find **Key Takeaways** and one **Action Item**. Like the **Pause and Ponder** breaks, these practical exercises are designed to solidify your learning and encourage you to apply the concepts before moving on to the next chapter.

This book is about how to initiate engaging conversations, develop deeper relationships, and create moments of genuine connection. "Tell Me . . ." invites curiosity, encourages openness, and allows you to step into any conversation with ease. It is the foundation of building character as it will change the way you perceive your value to others.

You will discover the necessary skills to "own the room" with a natural sense of ease. You'll learn how to use the ideas presented to navigate conversations, build rapport, and leave lasting impressions. With these tools, you'll be seen as congenial, smart, and confident—someone who knows how to make meaningful connections wherever you go.

Final Thought

Think of a conversation like a symphony. Your voice is the lead instrument—it sets the tone and rhythm. Eye contact? That's your string section, grounding everything with connection, inviting someone else to share their story. Inviting them to talk about their favorite subject—*themselves*.

Gestures and facial expressions? They're your brass and woodwinds, adding richness and texture. And the smile? That's your percussion, the heartbeat of it all.

When all these elements come together, a conversation becomes so much more than just words—it transforms into something dynamic, memorable, and deeply human. So, grab your conductor's baton and the sheet music and begin to orchestrate memorable conversations.

"A person's name is, to that person, the sweetest, most important sound in any language."

—*Dale Carnegie*

Chapter 1

Why I Wrote This Book

Let me share a story that changed the way I think about conversations—forever. It happened about forty years ago, and I can still picture it like it was yesterday. I was sitting in my living room, watching the CBS Evening News, when a segment came on about the opening of a new Broadway show. But this wasn't your typical Broadway production.

No orchestra, no elaborate costumes, no choreography. Just a simple stage setup: a row of chairs and a group of legendary actors passing a microphone, sharing stories from their lives in entertainment. They talked about their journeys in theater, radio, film, and TV—no scripts, just heartfelt reflections. It felt intimate, like you were sitting in their living room.

When the segment ended, the camera followed the actors as they left through the stage door. Outside, a small group of fans waited to catch a glimpse of their heroes. Among them were three older women, clearly excited, whispering and pointing as the actors emerged. And then, stepping into the scene, was none other than James Earl Jones.

You remember James Earl Jones. His presence was larger than life—Broadway royalty, the unmistakable voice of Darth Vader and CNN, a living legend. As soon as he appeared, one of the women couldn't hold back. She

Tell Me . . .

broke away from her friends, rushed up to him, and started gushing. She praised his voice, his talent, his entire body of work.

What he did next stopped me in my tracks. He didn't just smile politely or thank her. Instead, he leaned in, extended his hand, and, with a gentle smile, said, *"Tell me your name."*

Four simple words, but they were electric. "Tell me your name." Not "What's your name?" or "Who are you?" but "Tell me . . ." In that moment, James Earl Jones wasn't the celebrity towering over her. He was a human being, engaging with her as an equal. Those words shifted the focus completely—he wasn't just receiving her admiration; he was giving her his full attention.

That phrase, "Tell me . . . ," set the stage for a different level of engagement and stayed with me. It reminded me of something my dad used to say when he introduced me to people as a kid: "Tell the man your name, Son." Back then, it felt like simple manners. But watching James Earl Jones, I realized it was so much more. "Tell me . . ." is an invitation, a way of saying, "You matter. I want to know you."

This realization changed how I approached conversations—not just at work but in every aspect of life. Professionally, "Tell me . . ." became a tool I used to engage with colleagues, clients, and even strangers in the business world. But socially and within my family, it opened entirely new possibilities.

At a family gathering, instead of the usual small talk, I'd try something like, "Tell me about that recipe" or "Tell me what you loved most about that trip." Suddenly, the conversation would shift. People would light up, and we'd end up talking about memories, dreams, and experiences that might've never come up otherwise.

Socially, "Tell me . . ." became a way to connect on a deeper level. Meeting someone new? "Tell me what brought you to this city." Reconnecting with an old friend? "Tell me what's been inspiring you lately." It's a phrase that works everywhere because it's not about you—it's about inviting someone else to share their story. Inviting them to talk about their favorite subject—*themselves*.

As an executive coach, I started teaching this to my clients, many of whom admitted to struggling with starting conversations or keeping them meaningful. "Tell me . . ." became my secret weapon. I'd explain how it could break the ice in a meeting, build rapport with a team, or even defuse tension in a tough situation. But I'd also remind them: Don't save it just for the office. Use it with your spouse, your partner, your kids, your friends. It's a way to deepen relationships across every part of your life.

"Tell me . . ." isn't just another question—it's a gift. It tells the other person they're seen, they're valued, and their story matters.

James Earl Jones's simple act of asking that woman to tell him her name wasn't just about making her day (though it absolutely did). It was a masterclass in human connection. Those four words unlocked a world of possibilities for me, professionally, socially, and personally.

And now, they're at the heart of this book. Because whether you're talking to a CEO, a stranger at a party, or your teenage son, "Tell me . . ." is the ultimate conversation starter. It's an invitation to dig beneath the surface and discover something real. And in a world that's always rushing, isn't that something we all need?

Tell Me . . .

Before You Begin

Get the most out of this book!

Use this QR code or this link to download materials that will help you get the most out of this book and focus on improving your conversation skills.

https://www.fredreggie.com/readers-guide

Part 1
Why Conversation Is So Hard

"Everything is plainer when spoken than when unspoken."

—*Socrates*

Chapter 2

The Conversation Crisis

Cedric and Brianna had never been able to see eye to eye. Cedric was meticulous, a by-the-book professional who believed that structure and protocol were the backbones of success. Brianna, on the other hand, thrived on flexibility, believing that adaptability was the key to getting things done efficiently. They clashed often, exchanging passive-aggressive emails and tense text messages, each certain the other was impossible to work with.

One stormy Tuesday afternoon, a disagreement between them reached its peak. A client request had come in, and Cedric refused to budge on what he considered an essential policy. Brianna, frustrated by his rigidity, fired back over email. Their manager, weary of the ongoing tension, intervened. "Enough! Meet me in the conference room. Now."

Face-to-face, the conversation took on a different tone. They could see each other's frustration, hear the emotion in their voices, and, for the first time, recognize that they both had the same goal—doing what was best for the company and the client. By the end of the meeting, they found common ground and a new understanding of each other. The storm outside had cleared, and so had the tension between them. Symbolic? Perhaps.

Tell Me . . .

Why Are Conversations So Hard?

Despite our advanced technology, studies show that people are communicating less effectively than ever. A report from Robert Walters PLC found that 59% of Gen Z and millennials believe that instant messaging or email instead of calls or meetings is the best way to "get things done."[2]

The irony? While digital communication makes it easier to connect with anyone around the world, it's also making it harder to communicate with the person sitting right next to us.

So, why do we struggle with conversations?

⇒ **Fear of Awkwardness**—Many of us avoid conversations because we fear saying the wrong thing, dealing with uncomfortable silences, or misreading social cues. Social anxiety and personality differences (introverts vs. extroverts) play a significant role in shaping how we engage with others.

⇒ **The Convenience of Technology**—Texting and emailing provide a sense of control over our words and responses. Face-to-face conversations, on the other hand, require real-time thinking, emotional awareness, and vulnerability—things that can be intimidating.

⇒ **The Distraction Dilemma**—With constant notifications and endless entertainment at our fingertips, our attention spans have suffered. It's harder to focus on meaningful conversations when there's always something pulling us away.

⇒ **Lack of Practice**—Like any skill, conversation requires practice. If we spend most of our time behind screens, we become less comfortable with the nuances of real-time, face-to-face interaction.

You Won't Be Remembered for Your Texts

Think about the last time you attended a funeral. I've been to more than I'd like to count, and I've even delivered five eulogies myself. You know what I've never heard any eulogist mention in any of them? A meaningful text or email exchange from the deceased when she was alive. What people remember—what they hold onto—are the face-to-face conversations, the stories shared, and the moments of connection that left a lasting impact.

The same goes for moments of recognition and celebration. We remember the words spoken to us, the advice given in person, the laughter shared. It's the voice, the expressions, and the presence of the other person that make conversations truly meaningful. Digital messages may be convenient, but they lack the depth and emotional weight that face-to-face interactions provide.

The Decline of Face-to-Face Communication in the Workplace

In today's workplace, a staggering number of interactions happen via email or messaging platforms rather than in person. According to a recent survey I conducted among clients in 2024, nearly 70% of employees communicate with their colleagues primarily through email, instant messaging, or project management tools, rather than direct conversation. While these tools offer efficiency, they often strip conversations of their emotional depth and nuance, leading to more misunderstandings and less meaningful connections.

Adding to the shift away from verbal communication, Gen Z—who are rapidly entering the workforce—have been found to overwhelmingly dislike talking on the phone. Many prefer the perceived control of written communication, avoiding real-time conversations that require immediate responses and emotional engagement. This aversion to phone calls and in-person discussions contributes to a workplace dynamic where important issues can go unresolved for longer, and deeper relationships are harder to establish.

Why Push Through the Discomfort?

Despite the challenges, meaningful conversations remain one of the most powerful ways to build relationships, trust, and personal growth. When we push through the initial discomfort, we unlock benefits that no amount of texting or social media can replace:

⇒ **Stronger Relationships**—Trust is built through vulnerability, and vulnerability happens best in real-time interactions.
⇒ **Improved Conflict Resolution**—Misunderstandings are easier to resolve when you can hear tone and see body language.
⇒ **Greater Personal Growth**—Conversations challenge our perspectives, deepen our empathy, and expand our understanding of the world.

The Breakthrough: Choosing Conversation over Convenience

Returning to Cedric and Brianna—what changed? They didn't magically become best friends, but they did realize that no amount of emails or texts could replace an honest, face-to-face conversation. Moving forward, they made a habit of talking in person instead of relying on email, and their working relationship improved dramatically.

The lesson? When conversations feel hard, that's usually when they're most necessary.

The next time you find yourself hesitating to engage in a real conversation, try starting with two simple words: "Tell me . . ." These words open the door for deeper connection, making it easier to break through barriers and build meaningful relationships.

So, *tell me* what's holding you back.

Key Takeaways from Chapter 2

⇒ Openness builds trust.
⇒ You can enhance empathy and understanding by genuinely showing interest in others.
⇒ Face-to-face communication has irreplaceable value.
⇒ You can break down barriers by using "Tell Me..."
⇒ Tell me YOUR key takeaway:

_____

Action Item

Start a meaningful conversation today by saying, "Tell Me..." to someone in your life. Be fully present, listen without judgment, and watch how using this phrase transforms your connection. Write down how you felt in the moment and what you observed. Choose in-person communication over email or text in order to build greater empathy and opportunity for deeper understanding. Write down what makes conversation difficult specifically for you.

If you haven't done so . . .

. . . now would be a good time to download your Reader's Guide by using the QR code or clicking on the link below.

www.fredreggie.com/readers-guide

> "Start with Why."
> —*Simon Sinek*

Chapter 3

Don't Break The Rules

In Simon Sinek's bestselling book *Start with Why*, he emphasizes the importance of understanding the "Why?" behind any business, that driving force that defines our purpose.[3] We want to apply that same question—"Why?"—to understand the fear, anxiety, and apprehension of initiating and engaging in conversations. Why are we hesitant, fearful, and uncomfortable about initiating conversation—a fear that is not limited to engaging strangers but also extends to friends, colleagues, and family members? How is it we have become so afraid of stepping into the space of conversation? Do we think we will be critiqued? Will we come across as unintelligent? Do we question the richness, significance, or importance of what we might have to offer? My belief is that this fear is deep-seated and stems from our upbringing and the messages we receive during childhood.

Out of the Cradle and into the Spotlight

When babies are between twelve to eighteen months old, parents eagerly anticipate, encourage, and do their best to influence their first words, hoping for a connection to be made through "Mama" or "Dada." The parents celebrate these new words with joy, applause, and love, encouraging the child to continue growing her vocabulary. They constantly prompt her to repeat and learn new words, developing longer sentences each day. According to Mayo Clinic, "Between the ages of 2 and 3, most children speak in two- and three-word phrases or sentences [and] use at least 200 words and as many as 1,000 words."[4] Each new word or phrase warrants yet another celebration, eliciting smiles, laughter, applause, and accolades. So, it is easy to imagine what a cool thing this becomes for these kids. They are always on stage and *always* the stars of the show.

Encouragement continues as the child begins to ask questions and develop a persistent curiosity about the answers given to them by those adult family members. In fact, one of their great follow-up questions becomes "Why?" (Did they read Sinek's book?) Of course, parents and other adults try to explain the "Why?" only to receive another "Why?" for further clarification.

It continues as they interact with their friends—real or imaginary—and spend a lot of time talking to themselves. Have you ever watched a toddler playing alone and talking up a storm as he describes what he is building, organizing, or coloring? He is fully engaged and feeling comfortable in communication mode. No threats, no criticism, no restraint. Only continued encouragement from family and friends.

Then it all changes.

Around the age of four or five, despite efforts to showcase their newly discovered language skills, children begin to realize there are boundaries placed around speaking. When the chatter seems unending, they hear "Please be quiet, we're trying to watch TV!" or just an emphatic "Stop talking!" The child then begins to second-guess his own outgoing, effervescent, and colorful personality that once garnered the praise of everyone within earshot or on a FaceTime call.

Then a broader boundary is drawn around the child's impulse to speak and converse. Children are hit with a critical admonition that, possibly, alters their perspective on initiating conversation forever. "Never talk to strangers!" becomes an ingrained mantra along with the companion phrase, "Stranger Danger!" These admonitions, of course, are essentially critical. Parents and loved ones want children to be alert to the fact that there are—let's just say it—bad people in the world who can take advantage of their vulnerability and innocence. Add to those, phrases such as "Children should be seen and not heard" or "Never speak unless spoken to" and the impulse or desire to speak at all comes into question and is possibly extinguished. The idea that "silence is golden" also finds a seat at the table of conversational discouragement.

Include these messages as well, and the stage is set for life:

⇒ Don't speak unless spoken to.
⇒ Don't interrupt.
⇒ No talking in line, in class, in church.
⇒ You don't know what you're talking about.
⇒ Mind your own business.
⇒ Just be quiet and let ME do the talking.
⇒ Shut up! (And a dozen expletive-laden versions)

Suddenly, talking is perceived as a bad thing laden with qualifiers and uncertainty. We begin to question any value we might bring to conversation and dialogue.

All Shut-*tered* Up

When Emily was six, she was a whirlwind of creativity and curiosity. She loved to paint colorful pictures of imaginary worlds and would chatter endlessly about the characters and stories she made up. Her questions came fast and frequent, often about how things worked or why the world was the way it was.

Tell Me . . .

But at home, her endless stream of questions sometimes tested her parents' patience. During one family dinner, as she excitedly described the magical kingdom she had created in her drawings, her dad sighed and said, "Emily, can you just be quiet for a minute? Grown-ups are talking." Another time, her mom added, "You talk too much. Why don't you just sit still and listen for once?"

The words stung, and over time, Emily started to talk less. When she had a question, she thought twice before asking. Her stories became something she kept to herself, and the vibrant world she loved to share with others grew smaller and quieter.

School didn't help much either. "Stick to the topic," her teacher would scold whenever Emily's creative mind wandered during classroom discussions. One day, after a classmate laughed at an idea she shared, Emily decided it was safer to stay silent. She began holding her thoughts in, watching as other kids confidently raised their hands and shared their ideas.

As Emily got older, her hesitation followed her. At social events, she often lingered at the edge of conversations, unsure of how to join in. In team meetings at work, she stayed quiet, even when she had ideas she knew could make a difference. Years of being told to tone down her enthusiasm and curiosity had left her doubting whether her voice mattered.

Then, one day, during a brainstorming session at work, her manager, Marcus, noticed her scribbling in her notebook. "Emily," he said, smiling warmly, "tell me what you've got there. I'd love to hear your ideas."

Caught off guard, Emily hesitated, but Marcus's tone was encouraging. Tentatively, she began sharing her thoughts. As she spoke, Marcus nodded and engaged with her ideas, even encouraging the team to build on them. For the first time in years, Emily felt her voice carried weight.

That moment marked the beginning of a transformation. With each meeting, Marcus's consistent encouragement helped Emily regain confidence. Slowly, she started speaking up more, rediscovering the joy of sharing her ideas and seeing their impact.

It wasn't an overnight change, but Marcus's simple invitation—"Tell me . . ."—became the spark Emily needed to reconnect with the creative, curious voice she had once silenced.

> **Pause and Ponder**: Take a minute or two, right now, and write down some directives regarding speaking that were given to you as a child. How have they held you back in professional and social situations, possibly causing you to hesitate or withdraw from initiating conversation as an adult today?

These messages condition us all, as children, to remain silent, even though our earliest words were celebrated like the Fourth of July. Suddenly, our desire to communicate is met with boundaries and restrictions fixed deep in the recesses of our subconscious mind. This contradiction can lead to fear, anxiety, and glossophobia (fear of public speaking) throughout our lives, crippling and hindering our ability, or even our desire, to engage in beneficial and productive conversations.

Instructing children with phrases like "Never talk to strangers," "Don't speak unless spoken to," and "Children should be seen and not heard" can have lasting effects on their ability to engage in conversations and express themselves confidently. These directives, often meant to teach manners or ensure safety, inadvertently send a message that their voice is not valuable or that speaking up is inherently risky. Over time, this can lead to "conversational withdrawal," where the child becomes increasingly hesitant to initiate or participate in discussions, fearing judgment or rejection.

This form of withdrawal goes beyond mere shyness; it can create deep-seated self-doubt. The child may begin to question the worth of their thoughts and ideas, leading to a reluctance to share them with others. When a child is consistently discouraged from speaking out or is made to feel that their contributions are unwelcome, they internalize the belief that their voice is not important. This can erode their self-confidence and hinder their ability to communicate effectively in various aspects of life. Add to this the "face-to-phone" addiction (yes, it's an addiction) and you have the perfect formula for near-total social withdrawal.

Sidebar: For an in-depth analysis of how seriously detrimental phone addiction is to childhood development, read *The Anxious Generation* by psychologist Jonathan Haidt.[5] It's eye opening.

More seriously, these early experiences can contribute to the development of impostor syndrome, where an individual feels like a fraud despite evidence of their competence and accomplishments. (We discuss this in greater detail in Chapter 7.) The child grows up doubting her abilities and feeling undeserving of success because she's been conditioned to believe her input is not valuable. This profound self-image distortion can persist into adulthood, affecting personal and professional relationships, career growth, and overall well-being. Addressing this issue requires a shift in how we communicate with children, encouraging them to express themselves and validating their thoughts, which helps build a healthy self-image and fosters confident, articulate individuals.

Understanding this root cause is crucial in conquering our fear of initiating conversation. By recognizing these early admonitions and beliefs and breaking free from them, we can regain the confidence to connect with others in a more authentic and meaningful way.

Key Takeaways from Chapter 3

⇒ It is important to understand the root cause of conversational fear to address it effectively.
⇒ Encouragement and discouragement play a significant role in shaping a person's ability to engage in conversations.
⇒ The long-term impact of these experiences can greatly influence an individual's confidence in communication.
⇒ Overcoming conversational barriers is key to fostering open and effective dialogue.
⇒ Tell me YOUR key takeaway:

_____

Action Item

Take a moment to reflect on your childhood experiences with communication. Write down any phrases or directives that discouraged you from speaking up. Then, challenge yourself to reframe these experiences with a new mindset.

This week, make it a point to initiate at least one meaningful conversation. Use the phrase "Tell me . . ." to encourage someone else to share their thoughts and create a safe, open space for dialogue. Notice how this approach transforms both their confidence and your connection.

> "Technology is a useful servant but a dangerous master."
>
> —*Christian Lous Lange*

Chapter 4

The Conversational Cocoon

It wasn't that long ago—well, perhaps it was—when families sat on porches, neighbors waved from across the street, and conversations flowed as freely as the summer breeze. This was a time when storytelling wasn't confined to screens but shared in the warm glow of human connection—real person-to-person communication. The porch, the stoop, the sidewalk: These were our stages, the play was always in motion, and we were the stars of the show.

Fast forward to today. We've evolved. Or maybe we've devolved? Our open, vibrant dialogue has turned into something else—something quieter, something more insular. We've traded the symphony of social connection for the muted hum of "cocooned communication™." But how did we get here? And more importantly, how do we get back?

The Automobile: A Case Study in Isolation

If you want to understand how this metamorphosis began, look no further than the automobile. Before cars became commonplace, people walked. And in walking, they engaged. When you walked past someone, it

Tell Me . . .

was customary to say hello, and perhaps comment about the weather, or pay a courteous compliment to the neighbor or stranger. Walking was inherently social. We connected with one another.

Henry Ford changed that. With the advent of the Model T, the automobile transformed society. At first glance, it seemed to be an innovation that connected people. It allowed us to travel farther, visit more places, and experience more of the world. But here's the irony: It also isolated us.

Imagine driving through your neighborhood, safely ensconced in a metal shell. Your windows are rolled up. You can no longer hear the conversations on the street. You don't wave to your neighbors; you speed past them. The car, in effect, became the first mobile cocoon, offering freedom at the expense of connection.

The impact of the automobile on social interactions wasn't immediate or obvious. But over time, as roads were built and suburbs expanded, the distance between people grew—not just physically, but socially. The communal spaces where people once gathered—porches, sidewalks, stoops—became less central to daily life. They became places to *go* rather than places to *be*.

The car gave us autonomy, but it also gave us distance. And distance, it turns out, is the enemy of conversation.

Radio and TV: The Siren Song of the Living Room

And then came the radio. Then television. We invited them into our homes like trusted friends. They brought us news, entertainment, music, stories. But in exchange, we gave up something precious.

No longer did families gather on porches to swap stories. Now, they gathered in living rooms, facing not each other, but the flickering glow of a TV screen. The new hearth, the new storyteller, was a box in the corner of the room. The radio's soothing voice lulled us into a passive state. The television gave us color, but it also colored over the need for genuine face-to-face conversation. It pulled us into isolation as we sat next to one another.

We became spectators in our own homes. The firepit of collective storytelling was extinguished. And we let it happen because it was easier. More comfortable. The porch became an afterthought. The sidewalk? A place to pass through on the way back inside.

The Digital Age: Connected Yet Cocooned

Then came the internet. Social media. Smartphones. Each one was billed as a tool for connection. And on the surface, they were. We could text, email, like, share, tweet, and swipe our way through endless networks of friends and followers.

We could even build new neighborhoods with an infinite geographic footprint. But here's the paradox: While we became more connected, we also became more cocooned.

Real conversations—the kind where you could see the other person's eyes light up or frown in dismay—were replaced by "LOL," emojis, and GIFs. Face-to-face became face-to-screen. We traded richness for brevity, depth for convenience. We slipped away from engagement and into isolation. We began to live behind the glass, like prison inmates having conversations with visitors.

We live in a time where we can communicate with hundreds of people in an instant, yet we struggle to hold a meaningful conversation with the person sitting next to us. Think about it. When did you last have even a minimal conversation with the person next to you on a three-hour flight? Did you even initiate an introduction, an exchange of names? Communication has become a checklist rather than a cherished act. The porch of yesteryear has become the inbox. And instead of gathering in real-time, we're scrolling

Tell Me . . .

through endless feeds, searching for something to "like" but rarely finding something that moves us.

> **Pause and Ponder:** Stop here and consider how the smartphone has interrupted your desire for personal engagement and conversation with others. Write down your thoughts. Does anyone really stop to talk anymore? Or have we reduced our interactions to mere transactions? Swipe, click, done.

The Great Irony

Here's the catch: While we cocoon ourselves in cars, behind screens, or in front of TVs, there's a part of us that longs to break out. We miss the connection. We yearn for it. We haven't forgotten the magic of a good conversation, a heartfelt story, a real connection. But we've been seduced by the ease of disconnection. Connection is something we promise ourselves we will get around to one day when we have time.

We live in a world of irony: We're overwhelmed by options for communication, yet we're starving for genuine connection.

Sure, it's easier to text than to call. It's more efficient to send a voice note than to meet for coffee. But convenience comes at the cost of depth. We've automated the art of conversation, and in doing so, we've drained it of its essence.

Glimmer of Hope

But here's the good news. The same tools that have trapped us can also set us free.

Look around. Virtual reality, video calls, Zoom meetings—they're helping us rediscover face-to-face interactions, even across oceans. Mindfulness about technology use is becoming more mainstream. There's a growing recognition that maybe, just maybe, we went too far into our digital caves.

People are starting to realize that real conversations—the kind where you don't need an emoji to convey emotion—are irreplaceable. There's a movement toward reconnecting. To putting the phone down, looking someone in the eye, and saying, "Tell Me . . ."

There's a growing hunger for something authentic. And this is where the opportunity lies.

From Smartphone Cocoon to Conversational Butterfly

Janet never went anywhere without her smartphone. It wasn't just a tool for her—it was an extension of her being. Her thumbs danced across the screen as she texted, scrolled, and posted, seemingly glued to its glow. Her partner, Chandler, had grown increasingly frustrated. Their once-intimate evenings had devolved into silence, interrupted only by the tap-tap-tap of Janet's typing.

"Janet, I feel like I'm competing with your phone," Chandler finally admitted one evening over dinner. His voice cracked, and Janet looked up, startled, as though noticing him for the first time in weeks. The reality of his words hit her like a cold wave.

The next day, she decided to make a change. She powered off her phone and slid it into a drawer, a symbolic step that felt both liberating and

Tell Me . . .

terrifying. For the first time in years, Janet intentionally left her cocoon of technology and stepped into the world with nothing but herself.

It started with a simple walk. Without her phone to shield her, Janet noticed things she hadn't in years: the way the morning light filtered through the trees, the sound of neighbors chatting as they watered their lawns. She passed Mrs. Collins, the elderly woman who lived two doors down. Instead of waving absentmindedly, Janet stopped.

"Good morning, Mrs. Collins," Janet said, her voice tentative.

"Oh, Janet! How lovely to see you," Mrs. Collins replied, her eyes lighting up. "I was just thinking how quiet the neighborhood has become these days."

They stood there for twenty minutes, talking about the weather, the garden, and Mrs. Collins's late husband, who had once been the life of the neighborhood. Janet hadn't realized how much she had missed these simple human interactions.

Her most profound realization came a week later. She and Chandler had gone to a park for a picnic. Without her phone, Janet felt vulnerable at first, unsure of how to fill the gaps in conversation. But then, she asked him, "Tell me about your favorite childhood memory."

Chandler smiled, his face softening. He told her about summers spent fishing with his grandfather and how those moments had shaped his love for the outdoors. As he spoke, Janet saw a side of him she hadn't in years—a depth, a joy that their relationship had lacked amid the constant digital interruptions.

That night, as they packed up the remnants of their picnic, Janet felt something new: gratitude. She realized how much she had missed by burying herself in her smartphone. Chandler's stories, Mrs. Collins' laughter, the warmth of a genuine smile—these were the treasures she had forfeited for a glowing screen.

Janet didn't stop using her phone altogether, but she set boundaries. No phones at meals. No scrolling during conversations. Instead, she

The Conversational Cocoon

committed herself to being present, to engaging fully, and to saying, "Tell me . . ." as often as she could.

As weeks turned into months, her world expanded. Her relationships deepened. And, in turn, she noticed the impact her presence had on others. Mrs. Collins began baking cookies for neighborhood kids. Chandler started planning spontaneous date nights. Janet's own transformation seemed to ripple outward, bringing new life and beauty to those around her.

She had stepped back in time to reclaim something timeless: the magic of human connection. And in doing so, she discovered that the real power wasn't in her smartphone—it was in her ability to listen, to engage, and to bring her full self into every conversation.

The path forward isn't complicated, but it requires *intention*.

It starts with a small step: choosing to talk instead of text. Choosing to issue the directive "Tell me . . ." and to actively listen to the answer. Choosing to spend time on a porch—whether physical or metaphorical—and really engage with the people around you.

The solution to our communication problem isn't to throw our phones into the ocean or burn our cars. It's to reclaim what we've lost. To use technology as a bridge, not a wall. We must remember, however, that each of us has only one hundred sixty-eight hours in our week and we must be intentional in our commitment to fill more of those hours with meaningful conversation.

We can't go back to the past. But we can carry the best parts of it forward.

A New Dialogue

What if we made a new commitment? What if we started with just one meaningful conversation a day? A ten-, twenty-, or thirty-minute conversation where we REALLY listened. Where we weren't distracted by the dings

Tell Me . . .

and pings of a phone. Where we didn't cut it short because of a meeting or a deadline.

What if we brought back the art of storytelling—real storytelling, not Instagram stories or Snapchat streaks?

In this world of constant connection, we have the power to create something different. We can cocoon ourselves in silence, or we can break free and start talking again.

All it takes is one step. Two words: "Tell me . . ."

Are you ready to emerge from *your* cocoon?

Tell me your plan.

Key Takeaways from Chapter 4

⇒ We have moved from connection to isolation.
⇒ Technology has played a role in amplifying our social isolation.
⇒ Cocooned Communication™ has replaced the front porch.
⇒ We are living in a paradox of connectivity—not really connected at all.
⇒ Hope for reconnection lies in our desire, as humans, to engage.
⇒ Tell me YOUR key takeaway:

_____

Action Item

Take one intentional step today to break out of Cocooned Communication. Schedule a meaningful, distraction-free conversation with someone, even for just ten minutes. Put aside technology, look them in the eye, and start with the phrase "Tell me . . ." Notice how it transforms your connection.

"Tell me your name."
—*James Earl Jones*

Chapter 5

The Power of "Tell Me . . ."

Unlocking Connection in Every Conversation

We all struggle with poor conversation skills at times, like not being able to think of the right questions to ask or not remembering facts about people around us. Sometimes we start with closed-ended questions that result in one-word answers and conversations come to a screeching halt. It is critical to begin by making connections with those we want to engage.

Words create connections and understanding, and some phrases stand out as simple but incredibly powerful. One of those phrases is "Tell me . . .".

Think about it—there's a big difference between saying, "That's a nice painting," and "Tell me about that painting." The first just acknowledges, but the second invites a conversation, making space for deeper connection and engagement. Using just two words, "Tell me . . .," becomes a tool that sparks meaningful exchanges in every part of our lives—whether at work, with friends or within our families.

Tell Me . . .

When someone says, "Tell me . . . ," it's like an invitation to open up. You stop just observing and start sharing—your thoughts, your feelings, your experiences. It makes you feel heard and understood. That shift, where the person listening actively encourages you to speak, brings the conversation to a whole new level. It strengthens connections and deepens relationships.

Why "Tell Me . . ." Matters

Across different spheres of life, "Tell Me . . ." plays a transformative role:

Professionally:
- ⇒ **Building Rapport:** "Tell me about your experience with this project" breaks the ice with new colleagues, fosters trust with clients, and encourages valuable information sharing.
- ⇒ **Giving and Receiving Feedback:** Instead of a blunt statement, saying, "Tell me your thoughts on this approach" creates a collaborative environment where feedback is seen as a two-way dialogue.
- ⇒ **Mentorship and Coaching:** A simple "Tell me your goals" opens avenues for personalized guidance and empowers mentees to take ownership of their development.

Socially:
- ⇒ **Breaking the Ice:** "Tell me something interesting that happened to you recently" is a universal conversation starter that goes beyond small talk and fosters genuine connection.
- ⇒ **Active Listening:** Saying "Tell me more about your passion for photography" shows genuine interest, prompting meaningful conversation and creating lasting memories.

⇒ **Resolving Conflict:** When facing differences, starting with "Tell me how you're feeling about this" opens the door to empathy, understanding, and conflict resolution.

Familial:

⇒ **Strengthening Bonds:** "Tell me about your day" shows your loved ones you care about their experiences, fostering open communication and strengthening family ties.

⇒ **Uncovering Emotions:** When a child is upset, instead of making assumptions, say, "Tell me what happened" to create space for them to express their feelings authentically.

⇒ **Passing on Values:** "Tell me your favorite childhood memory" opens doors to share family history, traditions, and values, building a strong sense of belonging.

Mastering the Art of "Tell Me . . ."

The simple phrase "Tell Me . . ." has the remarkable ability to open doors to rich, meaningful conversations. It is an invitation, a prompt that immediately signals interest and a desire to listen. Unlike more direct or loaded questions, which can sometimes feel like interrogations, "Tell Me . . ." creates a space for the other person to share what is on their mind in their own words, at their own pace. This subtle shift from questioning to inviting allows conversations to flow more naturally, fostering a deeper connection between the individuals involved. As you begin to implement this phrase, you will see doors open that you didn't even know existed.

One of the greatest strengths of "Tell Me . . ." is its versatility. It can be employed by anyone, regardless of their age or comfort level with social interactions. For those who are introverted or shy, starting a conversation can often feel daunting. They might worry about saying the wrong thing or coming across as too forward. However, by using "Tell Me . . . ," even the most reserved individual can easily engage others. The phrase takes the pressure off the speaker to come up with a specific topic or insightful comment. Instead, it places the focus on the other person, allowing them to guide the direction of the conversation. This simple approach not only helps to initiate dialogue but also establishes the speaker as a great conversationalist—someone who is genuinely curious and eager to understand others.

Furthermore, it encourages openness and trust. When people feel they are being listened to without judgment or interruption, they are more likely to open up and share more personal or detailed aspects of their experiences and perspectives. This can transform an ordinary exchange into a memorable interaction, where both parties feel valued and understood. In professional settings, this can lead to stronger working relationships and more effective collaboration. In social and family contexts, it can deepen bonds and foster a sense of belonging.

My good friend, Dan, told me how shy his 8-year-old granddaughter, Olivia, was and how she was always buttoned up at school because she just didn't feel comfortable talking to other kids in her class. I shared the "Tell Me . . ." concept with him and he said he would introduce her to the idea. Two months later, Dan called me and said, "Olivia was shy at school, so we talked about using your two words, 'Tell me . . . ,'" to start a conversation with anyone. She won an award last year and again this year for 'Bear of the Month.' They are the Brownsville Bears and the award is given for academic achievement, kindness, and school community involvement. As her self-confidence grew, she became more outgoing and interactive with others in her school." Olivia is off and running, and she is a big fan of "Tell Me . . ." In fact, she even voted on the cover for this book. She liked the blue one that was ultimately selected.

Change the Flow of Conversation

During one of my coaching sessions with Eric, the conversation turned to the challenge of initiating meaningful interactions. Eric, a devoted father, shared his frustration about his relationship with his fourteen-year-old daughter, Jane.

"I don't know how to talk to her anymore," he admitted. "I ask her how her day was, and all I get is, 'It sucked' or 'Nothing special.' Then she's off to her room, and that's it."

I could sense how much this bothered him. Eric wanted to connect but felt stuck. That's when I introduced the idea of using "Tell me . . ." as a conversation starter.

"It's a simple shift," I explained. "Instead of asking a question that might feel like an interrogation, try saying, 'Tell me about . . .' and see where it leads. It's open, non-threatening, and shows genuine interest."

Eric nodded, willing to give it a try.

At the start of our session the following week, Eric walked in with an energy I hadn't seen before. He could hardly wait to share what had happened.

"You're not going to believe this," he said, sitting down with a big smile.

The night after our last session, Eric had been sitting in the den when Jane walked through the room, heading to her usual retreat upstairs. Remembering our conversation, he decided to try the new approach.

"Jane," he called out, "tell me about your day at school."

She stopped mid-step, turned to look at him, and, to his surprise, walked over and sat down next to him on the sofa.

"She just sat there," he said, still amazed, "and started talking. She told me about a group project in history, how one kid wasn't pulling their weight, and even this hilarious thing that happened in the cafeteria."

For fifteen minutes, they talked. Eric listened as Jane opened up in a way she hadn't in years.

Tell Me . . .

"It wasn't just the words," he said. "It was the way she looked at me. Like she actually wanted to share her world."

I smiled, knowing the power of such a small change. "What do you think made the difference?" I asked.

"I think it was my approach," Eric said. "I didn't push or pry—I just invited her to tell me. And she did."

Eric's story was a testament to how intentional communication can transform relationships. From that day forward, "Tell me . . ." became a cornerstone of his conversations—not just with Jane, but with others in his life.

Mastering the art of "Tell me . . ." is about recognizing the power of curiosity and the importance of creating space for others to speak. It's about becoming a better listener and a more engaging conversationalist, someone people feel comfortable talking to and seek out for meaningful discussions. So next time you find yourself wanting to connect with someone, try opening with "Tell me . . ." You might be surprised at the rich conversations that follow.

What Makes "Tell Me . . ." Unique and Significant?

While it might seem counterintuitive, starting a conversation with "Tell Me . . ." is surprisingly effective. Unlike questions that solicit limited closed-ended responses, like "What's your name?", "How was your day?", or "What do you do?", "Tell Me . . ." doesn't offer escape routes. It's an invitation that puts the ball squarely in the other person's court. It sets the stage for the other person to step up and engage while alternating between being the audience and being the performer. This phrasing subtly shifts the dynamic, turning us from passive questioners into active listeners and contributors.

"Tell Me..." primes us for engagement. By using a directive, we subconsciously commit ourselves to truly hearing the response. We're not simply fishing for a quick answer or waiting for our turn to speak. Instead, we're setting the stage for a deeper exchange, one where we're prepared to invest our attention in the other person's thoughts and experiences. This focused listening fosters connection and encourages the other person to share more openly.

Using "Tell Me..." effectively requires more than just saying the words. Here are some key principles:

⇒ **Be Authentic:** Genuine curiosity and interest in the other person are crucial. Your tone and body language should convey your desire to listen and learn.

⇒ **Be Present:** Put away distractions, make eye contact, and actively listen without interrupting. Show the speaker you are fully engaged in their story.

⇒ **Listen Actively:** Pay attention not just to words but also to emotions and nonverbal cues. Ask clarifying questions to show you're truly understanding.

⇒ **Reflect and Respond:** Acknowledge and build upon what you've heard. Share your own relevant experiences or ask follow-up questions to keep the conversation flowing naturally.

⇒ **Respect Boundaries:** Not everyone may be comfortable sharing deeply. Respect any hesitations and avoid pushing for personal information they may not be ready to share.

Transactional to Transformational

One of my clients is a major Fortune 500 service company whose sales team had always been transaction focused. For years, they operated like a well-oiled machine, closing deals quickly and moving on to the next client without skipping a beat. Efficiency and volume were the name of the game.

Tell Me . . .

But that all changed two years ago when leadership decided it was time to pivot—away from transactions and toward relationship development. The change made sense on paper, but the sales teams felt like fish out of water.

Suddenly, they were being asked to slow down and engage with customers at a more personal level. It was awkward, and conversations felt forced. These seasoned salespeople, experts at pushing deals across the finish line, were struggling to connect in meaningful ways. The very idea of developing relationships felt uncomfortable and, frankly, out of sync with how they were used to doing business. Besides, it was going to take more time.

That's when the simple phrase "Tell me . . ." started making the rounds within the teams. One account executive, feeling particularly stuck during a meeting, asked a long-time client, "Tell me, what's changed for you in the last year?" To their surprise, the customer opened up about their business challenges, personal struggles, and shifting goals. It was as if the floodgates had opened. The executive realized that asking a probative, open-ended question created space for genuine conversation. It was a revelation.

Word quickly spread. "Tell me . . ." became the go-to phrase, a key to unlocking conversations that went deeper than pricing and services. The sales teams began using it to learn more about their customers—their challenges, aspirations, and what truly mattered to them. And the results were nothing short of transformational. It began to create a distinguishing difference between the company and its competitors.

Customers started to feel heard, understood, and valued in ways they hadn't before. The more the sales team listened, the stronger the bond became. Loyalty to the company grew, not just because of the services they provided but because the customers felt a true connection to the people behind those services.

By shifting from a transactional mindset to relationship development—and using "Tell me . . ." as a powerful tool for engagement—the company saw an unexpected outcome: stronger, longer-lasting customer relationships that were built on trust. And in the process, the sales team discovered something even more valuable—how rewarding it could be to truly know and serve their customers.

Beyond Words

The power of "Tell Me . . ." extends beyond verbal communication. In every interaction, nonverbal cues play a crucial role. Nodding, maintaining eye contact, and offering encouraging smiles all communicate your genuine interest and create a safe space for sharing. Leaning in, having your feet pointing toward the speaker, and opening your hands as a welcoming gesture add the sincerity of your interest. (We'll delve more into non-verbal communication in Chapter 10.)

By incorporating these principles, "Tell Me . . ." becomes more than just a phrase; it becomes a philosophy of communication. It fosters empathy, understanding, and connection, ultimately enriching our professional, social, and familial relationships.

Remember, every "Tell Me . . ." is an invitation to explore, discover, and connect. Use it generously, listen deeply, and watch the magic unfold in all of your relationships.

Practice using "Tell Me . . ." in everyday interactions. Start with casual conversations and gradually work your way up to more sensitive topics. With time and practice, you'll be amazed at the depth and connection you can achieve in your conversations. It will become that second-nature quality that makes you stand out.

This is just the beginning of your journey to unlock the power of "Tell Me . . ." Remember, meaningful conversations don't just happen; they are initiated and nurtured with the right tools and intentions. Start asking, start listening, start sharing, and watch your relationships blossom!

In Part 2 you will see how to effectively step into the conversation space with confidence and comfort.

Tell Me . . .

Key Takeaways from Chapter 5

⇒ "Tell Me . . ." transforms conversations: This simple phrase shifts interactions from surface-level to meaningful exchanges by inviting others to share their experiences, emotions, and perspectives.

⇒ Practical applications of "Tell me . . ."
- Professionally
- Socially
- Familial

⇒ Intentional communication is powerful.

⇒ Non-verbal communication reinforces what is being spoken.

⇒ Tell me YOUR key takeaway:

_____

Action Item

Today, make it your goal to use "Tell me . . ." in at least three conversations. Whether you're connecting with a colleague, a friend, or a family member, start with "Tell me . . ." and actively listen to their response. Be fully present, show genuine curiosity, and notice how this simple phrase opens the door to deeper connection and understanding. Take note of how it changes the flow of your interactions and strengthens your relationships.

Part 2
Take The Leap

"If I were to remain silent,
I would be guilty of complicity."

—*Albert Einstein*

Chapter 6

Digging Deeper

Opportunities often slip through our fingers when we believe the lie that we should silence our voice. Just as oil, diamonds, gold, silver, and other precious resources are not unearthed by simply gazing at a vast, open field, the treasures of meaningful conversation are not revealed by remaining on the surface. Imagine a prospector standing at the edge of an untouched landscape, wondering, "Is there something valuable below?" Without the courage to dig nothing is ever uncovered. Sometimes the effort yields nothing; other times, it leads to striking pay dirt. But no discovery is possible without taking that crucial step of digging.

Conversation operates in much the same way. It is a form of excavation, a journey beneath the surface of polite exchanges and routine pleasantries. Yet delving into the unknown is not always easy. Fear of rejection, uncertainty about what lies ahead, or the comfort of staying in familiar territory can hold us back. Sometimes we must become comfortable with being uncomfortable in situations and reach out to those whom we might usually avoid engaging. That is where curiosity becomes our *conversational shovel*.

When we don't ask questions or dig deeper, we miss the chance to uncover the richness of someone's experiences, the brilliance of their ideas,

Tell Me . . .

or the foundation of relationships that could reshape our lives or careers. Insights, connections, and understanding remain hidden, buried beneath unspoken words.

Much like the earth's hidden treasures, the rewards of conversation await those who are curious enough to seek them. By asking, listening, and exploring, we uncover value that can surprise us—a deeper bond, an innovative idea, or even a renewed sense of purpose. It all starts with one simple action: engaging in meaningful conversation.

The conversation that follows is a powerful illustration of this truth—a testament to the profound impact of stepping into the unknown and the remarkable rewards that await when we dare to dig beneath the surface.

Emma's Epiphany

Emma was a general manager at a multibillion-dollar development company in New York. She was highly respected—everyone knew she was capable and driven, but she couldn't shake the feeling that there was a disconnect between the executives and middle management. She really wanted to find a way to bridge that gap, and honestly, she just wanted to have a meaningful conversation with the CEO, John.

Well, at the company's annual gathering, Emma finally got the chance. It was a rare moment since John usually only interacted with the executive team. But Emma, feeling confident thanks to some communication coaching, decided to go for it. She approached John, extended her hand, made eye contact, and introduced herself with purpose.

With a smile, Emma said, "John, I've always admired your leadership and vision for our company. Tell me, what drives your dedication to this organization?"

John seemed a bit taken aback, which, to be honest, was probably a nice change for him. He was probably used to the usual surface-level chit-chat at these events. But Emma's directness and sincerity really got his attention. He smiled back and said, "Thank you, Emma. I believe in creating a place where employees can thrive, where their ideas matter, and their voices are heard. I'm driven by the belief that, together, we can achieve extraordinary things."

Emma, not stopping there, asked, "Tell me . . . how can we, as middle managers, better support your vision?"

That question really connected with John. You could see his enthusiasm as he talked about how important it was for middle management to be involved in decision-making, to communicate effectively, and to collaborate. Their conversation ended up lasting for hours as Emma used that simple phrase, "Tell Me . . . ," to dive deep into what really mattered for the company's future.

Months later, Emma saw the impact of that conversation. A major project had been stagnant for months due to communication barriers that had been thrown up which stymied productive interaction between several departments. After her conversation with John, the collaboration between executives and middle management started to improve. There was a lot more innovation, and the workplace felt more dynamic. Emma's colleagues were amazed by how she had bridged that gap and had gotten the ball rolling on real change.

Honestly, that conversation became a turning point in Emma's career. She became known as someone who could spark important conversations and drive real change. It also showed her how powerful genuine curiosity and good communication can be, not just for her career but for the company as a whole. On top of that, Emma came to realize her true value as a conversationalist.

Tell Me . . .

It's Your Turn

Emma's story isn't just about a conversation—it's about daring to open the door when no one else even sees the opportunity. It's about the difference between standing on the sidelines and jumping in, between making a connection and leaving an impression.

Too many people wait for permission. They wait for the right time with the perfect circumstances or for the moment when they feel completely prepared. But moments like that rarely show up. Emma didn't wait. She created the perfect moment by using two simple words—"Tell me . . ."—to turn an everyday interaction into something bigger. She didn't start with her agenda. She started with curiosity, with empathy, with a willingness to see the world through John's eyes.

This is how change happens. Not by waiting for the perfect pitch, but by stepping into the conversation when others are silent. The power of "Tell me . . ." is that it invites more than an answer—it opens a dialogue, a genuine one. It's not about the question; it's about the signal that you're paying attention, that you care about more than just the surface stuff.

Emma's willingness to ask, and then ask again, showed John that she wasn't there to make small talk. She wasn't there to flatter. She was there to connect, to learn, to make something happen. She wanted to create an interactive and collaborative environment. And that's the kind of interaction that sticks. Because real conversations aren't transactions; they're transformations.

Real conversations go beyond the mere exchange of words—they create connections, foster understanding, and ignite change. When we engage authentically, we don't just transfer information; we shape perspectives, deepen relationships, and inspire action. A true conversation has the power to shift mindsets and open doors to new possibilities. It is in these moments of genuine dialogue that we discover common ground, build trust, and leave a lasting impact—not just on others, but on ourselves.

Digging Deeper

When you step into the arena with curiosity, the rules change. You go from being another name in the crowd to becoming someone who matters. Emma's simple decision to ask meaningful questions didn't just transform her relationship with the CEO—it shifted the company's culture. All because she was willing to engage when others weren't. Emma became a 10-foot "Waldo" in the room.

The takeaway? Don't wait for the right moment. Create it. Don't shy away from the conversation. Dig in. When you lead with curiosity and authenticity, you unlock the potential for real change. The kind of change that ripples out far beyond that initial conversation.

Because the truth is, in a world where most people are afraid to ask, real leaders are the ones who aren't afraid to listen.

As Nike encourages, "Just do it." Take a few minutes, right now, and walk down the hall and have a face-to-face conversation with a colleague. Or place a call to a customer or client and say, "Tell me what's going on in your world today." Afterward, write down how your conversation or call made you feel and what was the reaction of the person to whom you reached out.

Tell Me . . .

Key Takeaways from Chapter 6

⇒ Opportunities lie beneath the surface.
⇒ Courage to engage is transformative.
⇒ Tell me YOUR key takeaway:

_____

Action Item

Take a bold step into uncharted territory. Identify someone *outside your usual circle*—perhaps a senior leader in your organization, a community leader, or even someone you admire from afar—and initiate a meaningful conversation.

Start with "Tell Me . . . :

- ". . . about the challenges you're most passionate about solving."
- ". . . what inspired you to tackle that challenge."
- -". . . about your most surprising lesson along the way."

As the conversation unfolds, focus on understanding their perspective, motivations, and values.

Document your takeaways, then ask yourself how you can use this experience to approach future conversations with curiosity and courage. This exercise isn't just about one dialogue—it's about cultivating a habit of exploration that transforms how you connect with others.

"I still have a little imposter syndrome… It doesn't go away, that feeling that you shouldn't take me that seriously. What do I know? I share that with you because we all have doubts in our abilities, about our power and what that power is."

—*Michelle Obama*

Chapter 7

Overcoming Impostor Syndrome

Have you ever found yourself doubting your accomplishments or feeling like you've somehow "fooled" others into thinking you're more capable than you actually are, even though you've clearly earned your place through hard work and skill? It is likely that you may possess a degree of impostor syndrome.

Impostor syndrome is one of those psychological phenomena that, once you understand it, you start to see it everywhere. According to an article in *Psychology Today*, "Around 25 to 30 percent of high achievers may suffer from impostor syndrome. And around 70 percent of adults may experience impostor-*ism* at least once in their lifetime."[6] It doesn't matter if you're the CEO of a major corporation, a new hire at a startup, or a father trying to navigate a family gathering–impostor syndrome doesn't discriminate. It's that nagging voice in your head telling you that you're a fraud, that you don't belong, and that sooner or later, people are going to figure that out. It's irrational. It's deeply human. And, most importantly, it can keep us from connecting with others in ways that are both meaningful and necessary.

We like to think that conversation–whether in business, social situations, or family settings–comes naturally. It's a simple exchange of words,

Tell Me . . .

a back-and-forth. But for those plagued by impostor syndrome, this basic act of communication can feel impossible. It's not that they don't know how to speak. It's that they're convinced that what they have to say isn't worth hearing.

> **Pause and Ponder:** Take a moment now and write down a time when you had an opportunity to speak up but didn't because you felt there was no value to what you had to say, and you thought you would come across as insignificant and irrelevant. Reflect on what you wrote and find belief in your worthiness and the value of your thoughts.

The Power of Self-Doubt

Let's consider a typical scenario in the workplace. You're sitting in a meeting, and there's a topic being discussed that you know a lot about. Maybe it's a project you worked on directly or a subject you've studied extensively. But when it comes time to speak, you hesitate. Why? Because in that moment, impostor syndrome takes over. The thought that someone else in the room knows more than you do—or that your comment might come across as obvious or even naïve—keeps you quiet.

This hesitation isn't just a fleeting moment of insecurity; it's a behavioral pattern. The more you listen to that voice of self-doubt, the more you condition yourself to remain silent. The opportunity to contribute passes by, unnoticed by anyone but you. And here's the kicker: No one knows you're hesitating. To everyone else, it just looks like you have nothing to say.

Now imagine this happening in social or family settings. You're at a dinner party, and the conversation turns to a topic you're passionate about. But instead of joining in, you stay quiet, waiting for the "right" moment—one that may never come. In family gatherings, you might shy away from sharing an opinion because you assume no one will take it seriously or, worse, they will be critical of what you have to say. Over time, this pattern of silence becomes self-reinforcing. You begin to identify with it, seeing yourself as someone who's just "quiet" or "introverted."

But here's the problem: Impostor syndrome doesn't just keep you from speaking up. It keeps you from connecting.

Missed Opportunities

Every conversation you don't have is a missed opportunity. In business, this might mean passing up the chance to show your expertise or missing out on a professional relationship that could open doors. In social settings, it might mean never forming a connection with someone who could become a lifelong friend, mentor, or collaborator. In family settings, it could mean never fully engaging with the people who matter most to you.

What's fascinating about impostor syndrome is how it mirrors what psychologists call the "spotlight effect."[7] We vastly overestimate how much other people notice us. You might think that everyone in the meeting is scrutinizing your every word, but in reality, most people are too focused on themselves to pay that much attention to others. In a social setting, you might assume that everyone will notice your awkward comment or misstep, but they won't. And in family settings, where familiarity should breed comfort, we still let insecurity silence us.

Impostor syndrome is, at its core, a fear of exposure. You're afraid that if you speak up, people will discover the truth: that you're not as smart, experienced, or capable as they think you are. But here's the paradox—by staying silent, you're never giving them a chance to see your true value in the first place.

Breaking the Cycle

The first step to overcoming impostor syndrome is realizing that it's a story we tell ourselves—a story that can be rewritten. Think of it as a narrative that's taken root in your mind, one that you can challenge by deliberately engaging in conversations, even when the voice in your head tells you not to.

Take someone like J. K. Rowling, the author of the Harry Potter series. For years, she battled feelings of self-doubt and rejection.[8] It would have been easy for her to stop writing, to give in to the belief that she wasn't good enough. But by pushing through that self-doubt, she changed not just her own life, but the lives of millions of readers around the world. What if she had stayed silent?

Here's how you can begin to break the cycle:

⇒ **Shift the Focus**: Impostor syndrome makes you hyper-focused on yourself. Instead, focus on the person you're speaking to. Ask questions. Show genuine interest. When the pressure is off you, the conversation becomes easier.

⇒ **Reframe Conversations as Learning Opportunities**: Conversations aren't tests. You don't have to have all the answers. Instead, approach each interaction as a chance to learn something new—about the topic, the other person, or yourself.

⇒ **Start Small**: You don't have to dive into deep, philosophical discussions right away. Start by engaging in low-pressure conversations—small talk with a colleague, a brief comment in a meeting, or a casual chat at a social event. These small wins build your confidence over time.

⇒ **Acknowledge Your Expertise**: Even when you feel like an impostor, remember that you have experiences and knowledge that others value. Start by recognizing your own accomplishments, even if they feel insignificant. They aren't.

The Value of Connection

At its core, impostor syndrome is about disconnection—disconnection from your own abilities and credibility as well as disconnection from others. When we allow impostor syndrome to guide our actions, we miss out on the fundamental truth that conversations are the key to human connection.

Conversations create bonds, build trust, and generate new ideas. They are how we navigate the world in business, social situations, and family life. And the irony is, the more we let fear keep us silent, the more we reinforce the very feelings of inadequacy we're trying to avoid.

To overcome impostor syndrome, you don't have to be perfect. You just have to be willing to connect. To overcome impostor syndrome, just begin by saying, "Tell Me . . ."

Tell Me . . .

Key Takeaways from Chapter 7

⇒ Impostor syndrome is widespread but manageable.
⇒ Silence reinforces self-doubt.
⇒ Connection is the antidote to impostor syndrome.
⇒ Tell me YOUR key takeaway:

_____

Action Item

Take the first step in overcoming impostor syndrome by starting a conversation that matters. The next time you find yourself hesitating to speak up—whether in a meeting, social gathering, or family setting—challenge yourself to contribute by saying, "Tell me . . ." followed by a thoughtful question or statement. Focus on the value of the connection rather than the perceived risk of being judged and watch as the fear of inadequacy begins to dissolve.

"Wisdom is the power to learn something from everyone."

—*Ancient Proverb*

Chapter 8

The P-A-I-L-E-R Method

"I want to start a conversation, but I'm still not sure of the best way."

At one time or another, we have all felt this way. Uncomfortable, out of place, inferior.

American writer and self-improvement guru Dale Carnegie said, "First, take a genuine interest in other people. Genuine is the key word. Don't fake it. Train yourself to actually become interested in other people's lives. You yourself may be totally fascinating, but that doesn't mean you're the only one who's totally fascinating. Show people you understand that. Second, remember that a person's name is, to that person, the most important word in any language. Focus on remembering someone's name as soon as you meet the person. Use the name in your conversation so that you don't forget. Third, make the other person feel important—and do it sincerely. Once again, sincerity is the important thing. An ancient proverb says, 'Wisdom is the power to learn something from everyone.' If you want to be wise, if you want to be unforgettable, if you want to be a class act, find the important thing that you can learn from only one person—the person you're talking with right now. Fourth and last is a single-sentence principle: smile. What could be simpler? Smile. In fact, smile right now!"[9]

Conversations are the foundation of connection. Whether you're meeting someone for the first time or deepening an existing relationship, knowing how to navigate the intricacies of a conversation can set the stage for meaningful interactions. In this chapter, we'll explore a simple yet effective framework I created while working with clients on conversation techniques. This is a simple acronym that will help you master the art of conversation: **The P-A-I-L-E-R Method.**

Six Steps to Initiating and Maintaining Meaningful Conversations

Each letter of the P-A-I-L-E-R Method represents a crucial step—Prepare, Approach, Initiate, Listen, Engage, and Respond—guiding you through the process of initiating and maintaining impactful dialogue. Let's look at each step in turn. And don't forget to smile.

P - Prepare

Success in conversations often begins long before the first word is spoken. Preparation helps you enter a situation with confidence and clarity. Here are some ways to prepare:

⇒ **Understand the context**: Are you at a networking event, a family gathering, or a professional meeting? Tailor your mindset and objectives accordingly.

⇒ **Gather information**: If possible, learn a bit about the person you'll be speaking with. Knowing their interests or background can spark ideas for topics.

⇒ **Set an intention**: Think about what you hope to achieve in the conversation. Is it to build rapport, share knowledge, or simply enjoy a pleasant exchange?

⇒ **Prepare your energy**: Body language begins before words. A confident posture, a smile, and open gestures can signal that you're approachable.

The P-A-I-L-E-R Method

Remember, preparation isn't about scripting every word but about equipping yourself with the mindset and tools to start strong.

A - Approach

The way you approach someone sets the tone for the interaction.
- ⇒ **Close the distance thoughtfully**: Whether in a crowded room or an intimate setting, moving toward the person with intention signals that you value their attention.
- ⇒ **Maintain a warm demeanor**: A genuine smile and steady, welcoming eye contact create an immediate sense of comfort.
- ⇒ **Be mindful of timing**: If someone seems distracted or engaged elsewhere, wait for a natural pause to approach. Respecting their space conveys emotional intelligence.

Approaching with confidence and respect paves the way for a smoother initiation.

I - Initiate

Now comes the pivotal moment: starting the conversation. Here, the phrase "Tell me ..." can be your secret weapon.
- ⇒ **Introduce yourself:** Simply say, "Hello, I'm Javon Williams, tell me your name." This will immediately establish your interest in this person.
- ⇒ **Lead with curiosity**: Open-ended directives beginning with "Tell me ..." invite the other person to share about themselves. For example:
  - "Tell me about what brought you here today."
  - "Tell me more about your experience with [topic or activity]."
- ⇒ **Keep it light**: If the setting is informal, humor or an observation about the surroundings can ease tension.

A well-thought-out initiation demonstrates your interest and sets a conversational tone that's both natural and engaging.

Tell Me . . .

L – Listen

Listening is an active skill and arguably the most vital step in the P-A-I-L-E-R Method.

- ⇒ **Focus fully**: Eliminate distractions. Put away your phone and give the person your undivided attention.
- ⇒ **Observe body language**: Sometimes, what's left unsaid is just as important as the words spoken. A furrowed brow, a quick smile, or crossed arms exhibited by you or the person to whom you are speaking can provide deeper context.
- ⇒ **Use verbal affirmations**: Words like "I see," "That's interesting," or "Tell me more" encourage the speaker to continue.

Listening not only builds trust but also provides the clues you'll need to move seamlessly into the next steps.

E – Engage

Engagement transforms a dialogue into a meaningful exchange. It's about being present in every sense.

- ⇒ **Match their energy**: Reflect their tone and enthusiasm. If they're sharing something exciting, respond with equal enthusiasm.
- ⇒ **Ask follow-up questions**: Show that you're invested by delving deeper into what they've shared.
  - "You mentioned [topic]–Tell me how you got involved with that?"
  - "That's fascinating. Tell me more about what happened next."
- ⇒ **Validate their feelings**: Statements like "That must have been challenging" or "I can see why you're proud of that" foster emotional connection.

Engagement is where true rapport is built. It demonstrates that you value not just the words but also the person behind them.

R - Respond

A conversation is a two-way street, and your responses are just as important as the questions you ask.

- ⇒ **Acknowledge their input**: Reflect back what you heard to show comprehension. For instance:
  - "It sounds like that experience really shaped your perspective."
- ⇒ **Share authentically**: When appropriate, offer your thoughts or experiences. Avoid dominating the conversation, but don't shy away from contributing meaningfully.
- ⇒ **End with gratitude**: If the conversation concludes, thank them for their time or insights. Simple gestures like "I really enjoyed hearing your story" leave a lasting impression.
- ⇒ **Avoid contradiction**: Others take serious ownership of statements they make in conversation. If this is a social encounter, refrain from opening the door to potential conflict.

Responding thoughtfully reinforces the connection and ensures the conversation feels complete.

The P-A-I-L-E-R Method in Action

Imagine this scenario: You're at a networking event, and you spot someone you'd like to meet. Using the P-A-I-L-E-R Method, you:

- ⇒ **Prepare**: Gather your confidence and think of a few topics.
- ⇒ **Approach**: Walk up with a warm smile and eye contact.
- ⇒ **Initiate**: Say, "Hi, I'm [your name]. Tell me, what inspired you to attend this event?"
- ⇒ **Listen**: Be an active listener. Pay attention as they explain their reasons, noting their enthusiasm and choice of words.

Tell Me . . .

⇒ **Engage**: Follow up with a related question like, "That's such an interesting perspective. How did you first get involved in [their field]?"

⇒ **Respond**: Share your own thoughts about the event and thank them for the conversation as you exchange contact details.

With practice, these steps will become second nature, transforming every encounter into an opportunity for genuine connection.

By mastering the P-A-I-L-E-R Method, you'll gain the confidence to initiate and sustain conversations in any setting. Remember, meaningful dialogue is less about impressing others and more about being curious, present, and authentic. So go ahead—start with "Tell me . . ." and watch the magic unfold.

> **Pause and Ponder:** Take a moment to consider which of these six steps of the P-A-I-L-E-R Method are you most uncomfortable with. Write it down and commit to spending time pushing through the resistance you are feeling. What benefit will you receive?

Key Takeaways from Chapter 8

- ⇒ Preparation is the foundation of success.
- ⇒ Your approach to conversation sets the tone.
- ⇒ Active listening builds trust.
- ⇒ Engagement and thoughtful responses deepen connection.
- ⇒ Tell me YOUR key takeaway:

_____

Action Item

Put the P-A-I-L-E-R Method into practice at your next social or professional event. Start with preparation, approach someone with intention, and lead the conversation with a "Tell me . . ." statement. Build rapport by actively listening, engaging, and responding authentically to foster a genuine connection.

Part 3
The Science Factor

"It is not what we learn in conversation that enriches us. It is the elation that comes of swift contact with tingling currents of thought."

—*Agnes Repplier*

Chapter 9

The Neuroscience of Conversation

Why Talking Is Good for Your Brain (and Your Soul)

It's not just about the words. It's never been just about the words. When you sit down for a conversation—whether it's with a colleague, a friend, or a stranger—something remarkable happens. Sure, you're exchanging ideas. You're connecting. But beneath the surface, there's an entire biological symphony playing out. And it's rewiring your brain every time you open your mouth.

Let's get one thing straight: Conversation is not small talk. Real conversation is a workout for your brain. It's the key to unlocking empathy, building relationships, and, ultimately, increasing your emotional intelligence (EQ).

The Need for Social Interaction

Humans are inherently social creatures, driven by an evolved need for connection that is as vital to our survival as food, water, and shelter. This basic human need has shaped not only our behaviors but also our biology

Tell Me . . .

over millennia. Our ancestors relied on social groups for safety, cooperation, and resource sharing, which provided significant survival advantages. Evolution naturally selected for individuals who thrived in social environments, leading to biological changes such as the development of unusually large human brains. Anthropologist Robin Dunbar posited that our oversized neocortex evolved specifically to manage the complexity of social interactions and networks.[10] Neuroscientific research further supports this idea, revealing that our brain's default mode is social, always primed to prepare for the next interaction.[11]

The importance of social connection is underscored by the effects of its absence. Loneliness acts as an evolutionary warning system, akin to hunger or thirst, signaling an unmet need for connection. Studies using fMRI have shown that social isolation triggers brain activity similar to the cravings experienced when deprived of food, highlighting the profound impact of social disconnection.[12] This evidence reinforces the idea that our need for connection is deeply embedded in our biology. Recognizing loneliness as a critical signal, we should prioritize social engagement to nurture our mental and emotional well-being, just as we address physical needs like hunger and thirst.

The Brain: Your Ultimate Conversation Partner

When you engage in a meaningful conversation, your brain is doing some heavy lifting. Neuroscientists have discovered that multiple areas light up during a conversation—like the prefrontal cortex (decision-making), the amygdala (emotion), and even the brain's mirror neurons (which help you experience what the other person is feeling).[13] This interconnected web of neural activity is like a dance—each part in sync, responding, reacting, and building a connection with the other person.

But here's the kicker: *Your brain syncs up with theirs.* This phenomenon, known as *neural coupling*, happens when two people are fully engaged in a conversation. Their brain waves begin to mirror each other, as if they're literally on the same wavelength.[14]

It's like magic, except it's science.

What Happens to Your Brain During a Conversation

Let's talk chemicals.

When you have a real conversation, your brain releases a cascade of neurochemicals that make you feel good. They're the unsung heroes of connection, trust, and happiness. Here's what's happening behind the scenes:

⇒ **Oxytocin**: Often called the "bonding hormone," oxytocin gets released when we feel connected to someone. It makes us trust more and worry less. It's why we feel safe sharing our thoughts with someone we click with. It's also the reason why you feel closer to someone after an intense, heart-to-heart conversation.

⇒ **Dopamine**: This is the "reward" chemical. Every time you have a conversation that's engaging, interesting, or just plain fun, your brain releases dopamine. It's the same chemical responsible for that little rush you get when you check something off your to-do list or get a compliment. Conversation gives your brain a hit of dopamine, making you want more.

⇒ **Serotonin**: This one's about mood. Positive conversations raise your serotonin levels, which boosts your mood, lowers your anxiety, and keeps your emotions balanced. It's why after a great talk, you walk away feeling lighter, more optimistic, and ready to take on the world.[15]

Together, these neurochemicals form a cocktail that not only makes conversation enjoyable—it makes it *addictive*. Your brain loves good

Tell Me . . .

conversations because they feel good. It's like your brain saying, "More of this, please."

> **Pause and Ponder**: Think about the last great conversation you had. How did you feel in the moment and immediately afterward—physically, mentally, emotionally? Write it down now!

The EQ Boost: How Conversations Make You Smarter

Here's where things get really interesting: Conversations make you better. They build your *emotional intelligence* (EQ), the ability to understand, manage, and express your emotions while also being attuned to the emotions of others. EQ is the foundation of successful relationships, effective leadership, and personal well-being. And conversation is the gym where you work out those EQ muscles.

Here are some of the skills you'll improve from good conversations:

⇒ **Empathy Gains**: Conversations—especially the meaningful ones—help you develop empathy. As you listen, your brain's mirror neurons fire, allowing you to feel what the other person feels. This is empathy in action, and it's key to building trust and connection. Every time you practice it, you get better at it.

⇒ **Emotional Regulation**: When you're in a conversation—especially a difficult one—your brain is working overtime to keep emotions in check. Whether you're calming yourself down or reframing your thoughts, conversations are a real-time exercise in emotional regulation. And the more you practice, the stronger that muscle gets.

⇒ **Social Awareness**: The ability to track nonverbal cues, tone, and context—that's social awareness. Conversations train your brain to notice the unspoken parts of communication. You start picking up on body language, facial expressions, and subtle shifts in tone. Over time, you become a better communicator because you're more attuned to the signals people are sending.

⇒ **Self-Awareness**: Conversations don't just help you understand others—they help you understand yourself. When you talk things through with someone else, you're reflecting on your own thoughts and feelings. This process builds self-awareness, which is the foundation for personal growth.

In short, conversations are EQ superchargers. They teach you how to listen, how to empathize, how to manage your emotions, and how to connect with people on a deeper level. The more you talk, the more you grow.

Conversations Keep Your Brain Sharp

Here's the part most people don't realize: Conversations are also great for your cognitive health. Research shows that social interaction can help maintain cognitive function as we age. Think of it as mental cardio. When you engage in conversation, you're using multiple parts of your brain simultaneously—language processing, memory recall, problem-solving, emotional regulation. It's a full-body workout for your mind.

A study from the University of Michigan found that just ten minutes of conversation a day can improve memory and cognitive performance.[16] So, the next time you're tempted to zone out in front of a screen, remember that talking to someone—even for a short while—could be better for your brain than any app or crossword puzzle.

Tell Me . . .

The Bigger Picture

At the end of the day, conversations aren't just nice-to-haves—they're *essentials*. They're how we connect, how we grow, and how we become better humans. And the neuroscience behind it is clear: Meaningful conversation is one of the most powerful tools we have for improving emotional intelligence, building relationships, and keeping your brain sharp.

So what's the takeaway? It's simple. Have more conversations. Real ones. Not the surface-level, transactional kind but the kind where you actually listen, engage, and connect. Your brain will thank you. Your relationships will thank you. And most importantly, *you* will thank you.

Key Takeaways from Chapter 9

- ⇒ Conversations rewire your brain.
- ⇒ Neurochemicals oxytocin, dopamine, and serotonin are released in connection with good conversations.
- ⇒ Conversations are EQ superchargers of empathy, emotional regulation, social awareness, and self-awareness.
- ⇒ Conversations keep your brain sharp.
- ⇒ Tell me YOUR key takeaway:

_____

Action Item

After your next meaningful conversation, take a moment to become aware of how you feel. Do you notice a sense of connection, trust, or a mood boost? That's your brain releasing oxytocin, dopamine, and serotonin—the powerful neurochemicals that make conversations rewarding. To reinforce this awareness, jot down a quick note about how the interaction made you feel and why. Over time, you'll start recognizing the positive effects of real conversations, making you more intentional about seeking them out.

"When the eyes say one thing and the tongue another, a practiced man relies on the language of the first."

—*Ralph Waldo Emerson*

Chapter 10

What Your Body Says

When we take time to connect genuinely with others, it transforms our personal and professional relationships. While words are important, much of the connection lies in how we physically present ourselves. Understanding and mastering these non-verbal cues can unlock deeper, more impactful interactions, as expressed in *What Every Body Is Saying* written by retired FBI special agent Joe Navarro.[17]

Body language is a powerful, silent form of communication that speaks volumes before a single word is uttered. This chapter explores the key elements of non-verbal expression—how facial expressions reveal emotions, eye contact establishes trust and engagement, and posture conveys confidence or insecurity. We'll examine how gestures add emphasis and meaning, body relaxation signals comfort or tension, and even the manner of speaking—tone, pace, and inflection—can influence perception. Mastering these elements enhances personal and professional interactions, allowing you to read and project messages with greater clarity and intention.

Tell Me . . .

The Power of a Genuine Smile

A genuine smile is one of the most effective tools for fostering meaningful conversations. It conveys warmth, approachability, and interest in others. More than just a facial expression, a smile communicates that you are present and engaged, setting a positive tone for the interaction.

Imagine entering a room for a meeting or social event. A welcoming smile can immediately lighten the mood and make others feel at ease. It's a simple yet powerful way to create an inviting atmosphere. Pairing your smile with a friendly greeting—such as, "It's so great to see you," or "What a wonderful opportunity to connect"—further enhances the moment, signaling your openness and enthusiasm.

Eye Contact: A Gateway to Connection

Eye contact creates a connection that words alone cannot achieve. When used effectively, it conveys attentiveness and respect, showing others that they have your full focus. A calm and steady gaze builds trust, making the other person feel valued and understood.

In professional interactions, maintaining appropriate eye contact demonstrates confidence and sincerity. In social or family settings, it fosters a sense of closeness and understanding.

Combining a thoughtful question like, "Tell me more about that," with attentive eye contact communicates genuine interest, making the conversation more meaningful.

Posture: Communicating Openness and Presence

Your body language often speaks before you do. An open posture—facing the other person, shoulders at ease, and arms uncrossed—signals receptiveness and attentiveness. It shows that you are approachable and ready to engage.

Compare this to a closed-off posture, such as folded arms or a turned-away stance, which can unintentionally convey disinterest or defensiveness. By adopting a welcoming posture, you invite others to feel more comfortable and willing to connect. For example, leaning slightly forward while saying, "I'm glad you could join the party," communicates both interest and sincerity.

Gestures

Purposeful gestures enhance the message you're conveying, adding clarity or emphasis. However, too many or erratic gestures can distract from the conversation, making it hard for others to focus on the content of your message. Intentional, well-timed gestures can build connection and reinforce key points, making the interaction more memorable.

The Role of Relaxation in Conversation

Feeling at ease during a conversation is just as important as projecting warmth and openness. When you are relaxed, you create a ripple effect—your comfort naturally helps others feel at ease. This state of calm allows you to listen attentively, respond thoughtfully, and maintain a natural flow.

To cultivate relaxation, focus on your breathing. Steady, even breaths can help calm any nerves and center your thoughts. Pay attention to how you're sitting or standing: Avoid rigid or tense positions and instead aim for a balanced stance that reflects confidence without appearing forced.

Being relaxed doesn't mean being overly casual—it's about maintaining composure while remaining approachable. For instance, a slight smile, paired with a light comment like, "It's so nice we can all be together" can make the conversation feel more genuine. When you exude calmness, you help create an environment where everyone feels comfortable to engage deeply and authentically.

Upspeak, Vocal Fry, and Filler Words: Their Impact on Credibility

The way we speak carries just as much weight as the words we choose. In this section, we'll examine upspeak, vocal fry, and filler words—three speech patterns that can impact credibility, confidence, and how others perceive our message.

Upspeak

Upspeak, also known as "uptalk," is a speech pattern where statements are delivered with a rising intonation, like the inflection used when asking a question. For example, instead of saying, "I worked on the Carter Project," with a definitive downward tone at the end, someone using upspeak might say, "I worked on the Carter Project?" as though seeking validation or approval.

While upspeak has become common in everyday conversation, particularly among younger generations, it can unintentionally undermine the speaker's credibility in professional or formal settings. The upward inflection creates an impression of uncertainty, as though the speaker is unsure of their own statements. This can make it difficult for others to take the speaker seriously, especially when discussing critical topics or delivering instructions. It can also project a level of immaturity.

In business environments, where confidence and authority are highly valued, upspeak can signal inexperience or a lack of conviction, even if the content of the message is solid. To maintain credibility, it's essential to adopt a downward inflection for declarative statements, signaling confidence and finality.

Vocal Fry

Vocal fry, also known as "glottal fry" or "creaky voice," is a speech pattern characterized by a low, raspy, and creaky tone at the end of a sentence. It occurs when the vocal cords are relaxed and vibrate irregularly at a lower frequency than normal speech. While this voice quality is a natural register used by many speakers, particularly at the lower end of their pitch range, it has become increasingly prevalent in popular culture, especially among younger speakers and in media personalities. Some people intentionally use vocal fry to sound more casual or to even express authority, but its overuse can have unintended consequences in serious communication.

In professional or high-stakes conversations, vocal fry can undermine the speaker's credibility and authority. The creaky tone often conveys a lack of energy or enthusiasm, which can be interpreted as disengagement or even disinterest in the topic. Additionally, vocal fry can distract listeners, making it harder for them to focus on the content of the message. Research suggests that people perceive speakers with vocal fry as less competent, less trustworthy, and less employable, particularly in formal settings.[18] To avoid invalidating a serious conversation, it is essential to maintain a clear, dynamic vocal tone that conveys confidence and intention, aligning the speaker's voice with the importance of the message being delivered.

Filler Words

We've all heard them—"um," "uh," "like," "you know," "so," "actually," "okay," and "literally." These are filler words—verbal crutches that slip into our speech when we're thinking, hesitating, or trying to buy time. While they may seem harmless, their overuse can significantly impact the credibility of the speaker.[19]

Filler words dilute the clarity and authority of your message. Instead of making you sound confident and intentional, excessive "ums" and "likes" make you appear uncertain or unprepared. Imagine listening to a leader, a salesperson, or a keynote speaker who frequently says, "Um, so, like, what I'm saying is, you know, this is, like, really important." It's distracting, and it weakens the impact of their words.

Another common but often overlooked filler is ending statements with "right?" It's a subtle habit that can make even the most knowledgeable speaker sound unsure. When someone says, "This is the best strategy to move forward, right?" it invites doubt rather than reinforcing confidence. Instead of affirming a point, it turns a statement into a question, signaling uncertainty rather than authority.

Beyond distraction, filler words can subtly undermine the speaker's perceived expertise. In professional settings, where precision and confidence are valued, every unnecessary "uh" or "right?" chips away at credibility. People tend to trust speakers who communicate with poise, certainty, and a smooth delivery. When filler words pepper a conversation or presentation, they create an impression of nervousness rather than knowledge.

To reduce filler words, practice pausing instead of filling silence with unnecessary sounds. A well-placed pause adds weight to your words and gives the audience time to absorb what you're saying. If you catch yourself using fillers often, record yourself speaking, identify patterns, and consciously replace them with intentional silence.

A strong communicator isn't just one who speaks well—it's someone who speaks with purpose. Eliminating filler words is a small but powerful step toward ensuring that every word you say carries impact and credibility.

> **Pause and Ponder:** Where legal and for your own use, quietly and covertly record yourself while in a conversation. Listen to your voice inflection and voice quality. Is upspeak or vocal fry evident? Do you use filler words? Do you pause and actively listen to what the other person has to say?

Creating an Inviting Environment

The atmosphere you cultivate within your personal space plays a crucial role in fostering meaningful conversations. While the venue itself provides the backdrop, it is the warmth and intentionality you bring to your surroundings that truly sets the stage for effective dialogue.

Start with an inviting presence—your tone, body language, and choice of words contribute to the overall feel of the space. A warm greeting like, "I'm so glad you're here," or "I appreciate you taking the time to connect," instantly establishes a sense of welcome and ease.

The way you select your space also impacts the flow of conversation. Where you stand or sit can encourage face-to-face conversation as can the absence of unnecessary distractions. All help cultivate an environment where discussions can unfold naturally. Whether in a home, office, or shared space, the energy you bring and the details you shape make all the difference in making people feel valued and heard.

Tell Me . . .

The Takeaway: Be Genuine to Build Connection

At the heart of every meaningful interaction is authenticity. When you are genuine, your smile becomes more than a gesture—it reflects your true feelings. Your eye contact feels natural and sincere, while your posture and demeanor invite engagement. Above all, your sense of calm and ease transforms the conversation, making it an enriching experience for everyone involved.

By embodying openness, attentiveness, and a relaxed confidence in your "Tell Me . . ." conversations, you not only deepen your own relationships but also foster meaningful connections for those around you. These thoughtful gestures leave a lasting impression, enriching both your life and the lives of others.

Key Takeaways from Chapter 10

⇒ Non-verbal communication speaks volumes.
⇒ Relaxation enhances engagement.
⇒ Environment shapes dialogue.
⇒ Humor can add a layer of levity.
⇒ Tell me YOUR key takeaway:

_____

Action Item

Put the principles from this chapter into practice by planning your next meaningful conversation. Follow these steps:

⇒ Prepare your non-verbal cues: smile, eye contact, and posture.
⇒ Create a comfortable environment.
⇒ Use the "Tell Me..." approach: "Tell me about a time that was meaningful to you," or "Tell me what excites you most about this project?"
⇒ Stay relaxed and genuine.

Start by choosing one person you want to connect with more deeply. Put the call or meeting on your calendar. Use this framework to outline your approach and engage them with genuine curiosity and warmth. Reflect afterward on how these techniques enhanced the interaction.

"Wisdom is the reward you get for a lifetime of listening when you'd have preferred to talk."

—*Doug Larson*

Chapter 11

The Subtle Art of Listening

Active Listening

The phrase, "God gave us two ears and one mouth for a reason," serves as a timeless reminder of the value of listening over speaking. In conversations, the instinct to share our thoughts often overshadows the ability to truly hear what the other person is saying. This imbalance can lead to missed opportunities for connection, understanding, and even resolution in personal and professional relationships. The phrase encourages us to use our ears twice as much as our mouths, emphasizing the importance of being present and attentive to the perspectives of others.

Listening is more than simply hearing words—it's an active process that requires focus, empathy, and patience. When we prioritize listening, we demonstrate respect and genuine interest in what the other person has to say, fostering an environment of trust and openness. In a world where so many compete to be heard, the ability to listen can set us apart, making our contributions more thoughtful and impactful when it is our turn to speak. By honoring this principle, we not only deepen our relationships but also

Tell Me . . .

gain insights that would have been lost had we been too focused on formulating a response.

In a previous chapter, we explored how "Tell me . . ." creates an open invitation for conversation—an entry point for others to share their stories, experiences, and truths. But "Tell me . . ." is only the beginning. What follows is just as, if not more, important: *listening*. And not just any kind of listening, but *active listening*, the kind that transforms conversations into meaningful exchanges.

When you say, "Tell me . . . ," you've done more than ask a question. In fact, you haven't asked a question at all; you've set the stage for a deeper dialogue. Now, it's your responsibility to truly hear the response. It's a kind of contract: by inviting the other person to speak, you commit yourself to the full attention required to listen. After all, what good is an invitation to share if it's met with distraction or half-hearted engagement?

In this chapter, we'll dive into the subtle art of active listening. We'll explore why it matters, how to practice it effectively, and how it enhances every interaction by showing genuine commitment to the conversation.

Why Listening Is Harder Than You Think

Most people believe they're good listeners. After all, it seems like a passive task. You sit, you nod, you wait for the other person to finish speaking, and then it's your turn. Easy, right?

Not quite. The truth is *listening is one of the hardest skills to master*. Most of us don't listen with the intent to understand—we listen with the intent to respond. Even as the other person is speaking, our minds are racing ahead, formulating our next point or thinking about how we're going to relate the conversation back to our own experience. We hear words, but we often miss meaning.

When you say, "Tell Me . . . ," you're committing to more than just hearing someone's response. You're committing to understanding the story behind it—the emotions, the motivations, the context. And to do that, you must engage in active listening.

The Anatomy of Active Listening

Active listening requires intentional effort. It's not just a matter of letting words wash over you—it's about diving into the conversation, being fully present, and signaling to the other person that what they're saying matters. Here's how to do it effectively:

⇒ **Be Fully Present:** Active listening starts with presence. When you invite someone to tell you their story, you must bring your full attention to that moment. This means silencing distractions—both external and internal. Put away your phone, close your laptop, and resist the urge to glance at the clock. Internally, quiet your mind and resist the urge to jump to conclusions or judgments. Your focus should be 100 percent on the speaker.

⇒ **Pay Attention:** It's often said that "attention is the rarest and purest form of generosity." In today's fast-paced, multitasking world, undivided attention is a gift we rarely give. But when we do, it transforms the conversation. The speaker feels seen and heard, and their story unfolds with more depth and honesty. Their willingness to share amplifies.

⇒ **Listen with Your Body:** Active listening isn't just about what you hear—it's about what you show. As we discussed in chapter 10, your body language can communicate as much as your words, and in a conversation, it's a powerful tool to signal engagement. Lean slightly forward, make eye contact, and nod occasionally to show understanding. Small gestures like uncrossing your arms or tilting your head can make you appear more open and receptive.

The subtle cues you give with your body encourage the speaker to keep sharing. It says, "I'm here. I'm with you. Keep going."

⇒ **Reflect and Paraphrase:** One of the most effective techniques in active listening is reflecting back what you've heard. This doesn't mean parroting the exact words, but rather summarizing the key points or emotions to show that you're not only hearing the words but also absorbing the meaning.

For example, if someone tells you about a challenging project at work, you might respond with, "It sounds like that project really pushed you to think differently. Tell me how you felt at the end of it?" This not only confirms that you're following along but encourages the speaker to elaborate and dive deeper into their own experience.

Reflecting and paraphrasing create a loop of understanding. It allows you to check whether you've interpreted their words correctly and shows that you value their perspective.

⇒ **Ask Follow-Up Questions:** "Tell Me . . ." opens the door, but follow-up questions keep the conversation flowing. When you've listened carefully, asking thoughtful, specific follow-up questions can guide the conversation to richer places leading to the discovery of deeper context.

Suppose someone shares a story about a challenging time in their career. After listening, you might ask, "Tell me how you managed to stay focused when things were tough?" or "What did you learn from that experience?" These questions show you've been listening intently and that you're genuinely interested in understanding more.

Follow-up questions also give the other person permission to reflect further, often uncovering insights they hadn't realized they knew.

⇒ **Resist the Urge to Fix:** One of the hardest parts of active listening is resisting the temptation to jump in and solve the problem. Often, when we hear someone share a struggle or challenge, our instinct is to offer advice or solutions. But most of the time, people aren't looking for solutions—they're looking to be heard. Men are particularly guilty of this. It seems to be our nature to want to fix every problem. We tend to be the hammer always in search of a nail.

> **Pause and Ponder:** Which of these six listening directives do you find most challenging? Write it down and, next to it, write what you will do to overcome that challenge.
> Reflect on how this exercise made you feel.

When you respond too quickly with advice, you shift the focus away from the speaker's experience and onto your own. You disrupt the flow of the conversation, and, unintentionally, you may signal that you've stopped listening. Instead, let the speaker fully express themselves. If they want advice, they'll ask for it. Until then, stay in listening mode.

The Listener's Commitment

When you say, "Tell me . . . ," you've made a commitment. By setting the stage for discussion, you inherently commit yourself to the role of the listener. In that moment, *you are responsible for holding space* for the other person's words. And holding space isn't passive—it requires attention, intention, and empathy.

Tell Me . . .

This commitment makes you more attuned to what's being said because *you've invited it in the first place*. You've signaled that the conversation is important, and in doing so, you're far less likely to let your attention drift or your thoughts wander. It's a subtle but powerful psychological contract: by asking for the story, you've promised to stay with it until the end.

The Impact of Active Listening

When you truly listen, you create trust. The other person feels safe to share more because they know their words matter. Conversations become more authentic, and the connection deepens. In interviews, active listening reveals layers of motivation, personality, and character that might otherwise remain hidden. In performance reviews, it fosters growth by showing employees that their voices are valued. In friendships and family conversations, it strengthens bonds, leading to more meaningful relationships.

Active listening changes the entire dynamic of communication. It shifts the focus from simply exchanging information to building understanding.

Sophia's Dilemma

Isaac adjusted his chair and glanced at his schedule for the day. It was packed, as usual, but the next meeting stood out—his one-on-one with Sophia, a promising but relatively new project manager on his team. When she entered his office, Isaac immediately noticed that something was off. Sophia's usual confident demeanor was absent; instead, she clutched her notebook tightly, her shoulders slightly slumped, and her gaze fixed on the floor.

"Good to see you, Sophia," Isaac said warmly, gesturing for her to take a seat. "Tell me what's on your mind today?"

The Subtle Art of Listening

Sophia hesitated, flipping through her notebook. Isaac stayed quiet, giving her the space to gather her thoughts. Finally, she looked up and said, "It's the Carter Project. I'm struggling."

Isaac nodded, encouraging her to continue without interruption.

"I feel like I'm spinning my wheels," Sophia said, her voice tinged with frustration. "The team isn't meeting deadlines, and I'm not sure if it's because I'm not managing them effectively or if there's something else going on. It's starting to feel overwhelming."

Isaac leaned back slightly, maintaining eye contact while keeping his posture open and nonjudgmental. He could sense there was more beneath the surface, so he simply asked, "Tell me more about what you're seeing with the team. What do you think is causing the delays?"

That question opened the door. Sophia began outlining the issues: unclear responsibilities among team members, breakdowns in communication during the last two sprints, and her own struggle to balance technical oversight with team leadership.

Isaac listened carefully, nodding occasionally and jotting down a few notes to ensure he fully understood. When she paused, he didn't rush to offer solutions. Instead, he summarized what he'd heard: "It sounds like you're juggling a lot—trying to manage both the technical demands of the project and the dynamics of the team—and it's leaving you feeling stuck. Does that capture it?"

Sophia's shoulders relaxed, and she nodded. "Yes, that's exactly it. Thank you for understanding."

Rather than offering a quick fix, Isaac asked, "Tell me what you think could help the team regain clarity and momentum. You know the team better than anyone."

Sophia thought for a moment before suggesting a workshop to realign her team on roles and expectations. She also proposed delegating some of the technical oversight to her senior developer, freeing herself to focus on team communication and leadership.

Tell Me . . .

Isaac smiled. "Those are excellent ideas, Sophia. Let's map out a plan together to put these changes in motion. And if you ever feel stuck like this again, don't hesitate to talk it through with me. Sometimes just articulating the challenges can make all the difference."

By the end of the meeting, Sophia seemed noticeably lighter, her confidence visibly restored. Over the next few weeks, the Carter Project made significant progress, meeting its deadlines and delivering results. Sophia later shared with Isaac how much it had meant to her to feel heard during that conversation.

For Isaac, the experience was a reminder of the impact of active listening. By creating a space where Sophia could share openly, he empowered her to uncover her own solutions. Sometimes, he realized, leadership isn't about having all the answers but about being present, listening deeply, and guiding others toward their potential.

Listening as a Superpower

We live in a world where everyone is rushing to be heard and the ability to truly listen stands out. It's a superpower that few possess but all recognize when they encounter it. Active listening is a tool that not only enhances conversations but also elevates your relationships, your leadership, and your ability to connect on a deeper level.

The subtle art of listening, paired with the power of "Tell me . . ." creates a foundation for conversations that matter. These aren't fleeting exchanges but meaningful discussions that leave a lasting impact.

Key Takeaways from Chapter 11

⇒ Active listening requires intentional effort.
⇒ Listening is understanding, not responding.
⇒ Reflect, paraphrase, and ask follow-up questions.
⇒ Resist the urge to solve problems.
⇒ Tell me YOUR key takeaway:

_____

Action Item

Commit to practicing active listening today. Choose one interaction—whether personal or professional—and apply the principles of presence, attention, and reflection. Resist distractions, paraphrase what you hear, and ask a follow-up question to deepen the exchange. Notice how this transforms the quality of the conversation and strengthens your connection with the other person.

"The most important thing in communication is hearing what isn't said."

—*Peter Drucker*

Chapter 12

Listening Between The Lines

What Isn't Said

In the last chapter, we focused on the importance of active listening—the kind of attention that transforms conversations into meaningful exchanges. But to truly master the art of listening, we must go even deeper. *It's not just about what is said, but how it's said.* The words we choose are only a fraction of the communication.

When you invite someone to "Tell me . . . ," you're not just opening the door to words—you're opening the door to the full range of their communication. And sometimes, the most important parts of that communication are the things they aren't saying outright. In this chapter, we'll discover other subtle cues that reveal the full truth of what someone is communicating.

The Power of Voice Inflection

We've all experienced it: Someone says, "I'm fine," but their voice betrays them. There's something in the way they say the words—the flatness of their tone, the hesitation before they speak—that makes you question the truth behind them. This is the power of *voice inflection*. It's not just about the words someone chooses; it's about how those words are delivered.

Inflection can completely change the meaning of a sentence. Consider the phrase, "I didn't say you stole the money." Depending on which word is emphasized, this simple sentence can have six completely different meanings:

⇒ *I* didn't say you stole the money. (Someone else did.)
⇒ I *didn't* say you stole the money. (I implied it, but didn't say it.)
⇒ I didn't *say* you stole the money. (I might have written it down or hinted at it.)
⇒ I didn't say *you* stole the money. (Someone else stole it.)
⇒ I didn't say you *stole* the money. (You may have borrowed it.)
⇒ I didn't say you stole the *money*. (You took something else.)

The words stay the same, but the meaning shifts entirely based on which word is emphasized. This is why *listening to voice inflection* is so critical—it reveals the true meaning behind the words.

When someone responds to a question like "Tell me about your biggest challenge," they may start by saying, "Well, it wasn't that big of a deal..." But pay attention to the rising inflection at the end of the sentence. Are they questioning their own words? Is there tension in their voice that suggests the challenge was, in fact, significant? Sometimes, the truth is hidden in the tone of the response, not the content.

To be a master listener, you must train yourself to listen to more than just the words being spoken. Listen for the shifts in tone, the subtle rises and falls in pitch that signal emotion. Is the speaker excited, but trying to play it down? Are they disappointed, but masking it with professionalism? These nuances often tell you more than the words themselves.

The Unspoken Cues of Body Language

Alongside voice inflection, *body language* is one of the most powerful forms of non-verbal communication. In 1971, Dr. Albert Mehrabian, a professor at UCLA, published a book called *Silent Messages*. He claimed that 93 percent of what we say to people, we say without words; more specifically, 55 percent of communication is done through body language and 38 percent through tone. This includes gestures, facial expressions, posture, and eye contact. Only the remaining seven percent of what we say is said with spoken words.[20] When you invite someone to share their story, their body often tells a parallel story that words alone cannot capture.

Imagine you're in a job interview, and you ask a candidate to "Tell me about a time you faced a difficult decision." They start speaking confidently, but as they do, their posture stiffens. They cross their arms tightly across their chest, and their eyes dart down to the floor. While their words may be polished, their body language suggests discomfort or unease.

Crossed arms, for instance, can signal defensiveness or a need to protect oneself. A downcast gaze may indicate avoidance, while shifting in a chair can suggest nervousness or impatience. On the other hand, an open posture—relaxed arms, steady eye contact, and forward-leaning body—signals engagement, trust, and comfort.

What's critical here is learning to *listen with your eyes as much as your ears*. Words tell you what someone *wants* you to hear, but body language tells you what they *feel*. Pay attention to the incongruence between words and gestures. If someone is telling you they're excited but their body is slumped and their hands are motionless, something is off. If they say they're fine, but their eyes avoid yours, there's more to the story.

Tell Me . . .

> **Pause and Ponder:** Take a few minutes to think about your body language when you are in an uncomfortable situation. Do you cross your arms? Do you slump? Are your hands in your pockets? Do you rock side-to-side?
>
> How do you plan to overcome body language that is not conducive to productive conversation?

The Executive's Story: A High-Stakes Decision Based on Non-Verbal Cues

Corporate leadership is demanding. The stakes are often high, and decisions carry weight. Cynthia, a newly appointed CEO, found herself in such a situation during a pivotal board meeting. The company was considering a merger that, on paper, seemed like a perfect fit. The financials lined up, and strategic synergies were evident. Yet, as the meeting progressed, Cynthia picked up on a subtle shift in the room's energy.

During the final presentation, a senior executive who had been a strong advocate for the merger appeared uncharacteristically tense. His posture became rigid, his arms crossed tightly over his chest, and his eyes began darting around the room. Something was clearly bothering him.

After the presentations, Cynthia invited discussion, and while most board members spoke in favor of moving forward with the merger, the normally vocal senior executive remained unusually quiet. Sensing hesitation, Cynthia paused the meeting and asked to speak with him privately.

In their conversation, Cynthia chose not to press for answers immediately. Instead, she mirrored the same attentiveness she'd demonstrated in the boardroom, allowing him to speak when ready. Finally, he shared his concerns about the cultural fit between the two companies. While the financials were sound, he had observed tension and unease in preliminary meetings with the other firm's leadership. Cynthia's ability to read his non-verbal signals had uncovered an issue that words hadn't revealed—an issue that, if left unaddressed, could have jeopardized the merger.

By trusting her instincts and paying attention to the non-verbal cues in the room, Cynthia reopened the conversation with the board and steered the company away from what could have been a costly mistake.

Family Dynamics: Understanding Non-Verbal Cues at Home

Non-verbal communication also plays a pivotal role in family dynamics, where emotions often run high. In these intimate settings, body language and unspoken signals can reveal far more than words ever could.

Consider a family dinner where everyone is gathered around the table. As the meal begins, you notice that your teenage daughter, usually talkative, is unusually quiet. She picks at her food, her shoulders slumped, her gaze fixed on her plate. No words are exchanged, but her body language is communicating volumes. Something is wrong.

Later that evening, you gently ask her if something is bothering her. Initially hesitant, she eventually opens up about a tough day at school and a disagreement with a friend. Without her ever saying a word, you had already sensed her distress. This is the power of reading body language in family settings. It allows us to tune into the emotional undercurrents of our loved ones, even when they're not ready to voice their feelings.

Tell Me . . .

The Weight of Silence

Sometimes, the loudest part of a conversation is the silence that fills it. *Pauses, hesitations, and quiet moments* often speak volumes.

When you say, "Tell Me . . ." and the person takes a long pause before responding, that pause is significant. It might mean they're reflecting deeply, that the question struck an emotional chord, or that they're considering how much to reveal. Silence can be an invitation to dig deeper, but only if you're patient enough to allow it to linger.

In Western cultures, many of us are uncomfortable with silence in conversation. We rush to fill the gaps, thinking that the conversation has stalled. But often, silence is where the real thinking happens. If someone pauses for a long time before responding, don't rush in to fill the space. Let the silence breathe. In that stillness, the speaker is often processing something more profound than they would have shared had you interrupted.

When you do speak again, acknowledge the pause. You might say, "I noticed you took a moment there. Tell me what came to mind during that pause." This not only gives them the opportunity to reflect but shows that you're attuned to the rhythm of the conversation.

Listening for Emotion

People rarely communicate emotions directly. Instead, we often express them through tones, gestures, and indirect language. As a listener, your task is to pick up on these emotional cues and respond to them with empathy and understanding.

For example, when someone says, "I guess it was no big deal," but their voice drops and they avert their gaze, you're hearing more than just a statement. You're hearing disappointment, or perhaps frustration, lurking beneath the surface. The emotional reality isn't found in the literal words, but in how they're delivered.

This is where *empathy* becomes a critical part of listening. You're not just processing the information you're given—you're connecting with the emotions behind that information. If someone's voice cracks while they recount a challenge, you recognize that vulnerability and respond accordingly. If they speed through an answer with a forced brightness, you pick up on the avoidance and gently probe deeper.

By listening for emotion, you go beyond the transactional level of communication. You're no longer just gathering facts—you're building understanding.

Crafting Your Responses Based on What's Unsaid

Listening between the lines isn't just about picking up on subtle cues—it's about responding to them. Once you've attuned yourself to the layers of communication beyond words, your responses can become more insightful and empathetic.

For instance, if someone says, "It was a challenging project, but we got through it," with a strained smile and clenched hands, you might follow up with, "It sounds like there were moments when things didn't go as planned. Tell me about those." By doing this, you're not just taking their words at face value—you're acknowledging the tension you sensed and inviting them to share the full picture.

Likewise, if someone pauses for an unusually long time before answering a question, you might say, "It seems like that question gave you pause. I'd love to hear what's on your mind." This response tells them that you're not rushing through the conversation, and you're genuinely interested in the deeper layers of their experience.

Tell Me . . .

Reading Between the Lines: The Listener's Superpower

As you develop the ability to listen between the lines, you gain a kind of superpower. You're no longer just hearing words—you're decoding the full range of human communication. You understand that a person's true meaning isn't always found in the literal sense of what they say, but in how they say it. And in that understanding lies the key to deeper connections, more meaningful conversations, and richer relationships.

"Tell Me . . ." invites someone to share their story. But *how* you listen to that story is where the magic happens. Listen for the voice inflection that shifts the meaning of a sentence. Watch for the body language that contradicts the spoken word. Embrace the silences that allow thoughts to settle and emotions to rise. And, most importantly, respond with empathy to what isn't being said aloud.

When you master the art of listening between the lines, you're no longer just having conversations—you're uncovering the true heart of communication.

Key Takeaways from Chapter 12

⇒ Listening isn't just about hearing words.
⇒ Voice inflection and the way words are delivered change their entire meaning.
⇒ Body language tells a parallel story.
⇒ Pauses and moments of quiet hold significant meaning.
⇒ Responding with empathy to emotional cues creates deeper conversation.
⇒ Tell me YOUR key takeaways:

_____

Action Item

The next time you engage in a conversation, practice listening between the lines. Pay close attention to voice inflections, body language, and moments of silence. When you sense something unspoken, respond with curiosity and empathy using the phrase, "Tell me more about that." This will transform your conversations into moments of true connection and understanding.

"People's minds are changed through observation and not through argument."

—*Will Rogers*

Chapter 13

The Power of Observation

Noticing Little Things Sparks Great Conversations

Some of the best conversations don't start with profound questions or thought-provoking insights. They begin with something simple—something *noticed*. The act of paying attention, of truly seeing the world around you and the details that others often miss, is a powerful tool for building connections. Being observant allows you to open a conversation not just with words but with curiosity, empathy, and genuine interest in the person you're engaging with.

In this chapter, we'll explore how *observation*—whether it's the photos on someone's wall, the trophies on their desk, or even the clothes they're wearing—can help you initiate conversations that are not only more authentic but also more personal and engaging.

Why Observation Matters

When we enter a room or meet someone for the first time, most of us are focused on what we're going to say. We're preoccupied with making a good

Tell Me . . .

impression, finding the right words, or navigating the conversation. But what if, instead, you started by *paying attention to your surroundings* and the subtle cues the other person is already giving you through how they've arranged their space?

The things people choose to display—their office décor, the books on their shelves, their clothing, or the objects on their desk—are often clues to what they value, where they've been, and what's important to them. By taking the time to notice these things, you gain immediate insight into their world, and you can use that insight to start a meaningful conversation.

The key here is that *observation shifts the focus*. Instead of coming into a conversation thinking about yourself or your agenda, you start by focusing on the other person and the details of their environment. This simple act of looking closely and noticing what's around you opens up opportunities to connect on a deeper level.

Starting with What You See

Imagine you walk into someone's office for a meeting. There are a million ways to begin the conversation, but starting with what you see allows you to anchor the dialogue in something tangible. Perhaps you notice a framed photo of them standing at the finish line of a marathon, or maybe there's a trophy for an industry award proudly displayed on a shelf. Each of these details is a potential doorway into a richer conversation.

Here are some examples of how to turn your observations into conversation starters:

- ⇒ **Photos**: "I noticed the photo on your desk of you hiking. Tell me where that was taken. It looks like an incredible spot."
- ⇒ **Trophies/Awards**: "That's an impressive award. Tell me about the project that earned you that recognition."

⇒ **Books**: "I see you've got a copy of *[book title]*. I've heard great things about it—tell me what you think."
⇒ **Personal Items**: "I love the baseball signed by [player's name]. Tell me the story behind that."

These are simple, surface-level observations, but they open the door for deeper conversations. The person's response will likely lead into more personal territory—sharing stories of their hobbies, passions, or achievements. And because you started with something *you noticed*, the conversation feels natural and authentic.

The Magic of Personal Details

People display certain things in their personal or professional spaces for a reason. Those objects—whether they're photos, artwork, or memorabilia—are usually tied to experiences or values they care deeply about. *Noticing those details is a way of showing respect* for their personal story. It says, "I see you, and I'm interested in learning more about what makes you, you."

Imagine walking into an office and seeing a collection of family photos. You could ask, "That looks like a wonderful family photo—tell me where that was taken." Suddenly, you're no longer just engaging in small talk. You've opened the door for the other person to share something that's meaningful to them. It turns a generic conversation into one that's personal, even intimate.

When you observe and comment on these details, you're signaling that you're genuinely interested in the person behind the title or the job. This helps build rapport and establishes a foundation of trust, which leads to more open and authentic conversations.

Tell Me . . .

> **Pause and Ponder:** Stop and look around the room. Imagine you are in a client's office or a friend's home. What do you see? Among the items you see, which ones could be helpful in beginning a conversation? What would be your opening phrase to get a conversation in motion?

How to Sharpen Your Observational Skills

Observation, like any skill, can be developed. Some people are naturally attuned to the details around them, while others need to practice paying attention. If you want to become better at using observation to spark great conversations, here are a few techniques:

⇒ **Take a Moment to Scan the Room:** Before diving into the conversation, take a moment to scan your surroundings. Look at the objects in the room—photos, artwork, plaques, awards, or even the way the space is organized. Ask yourself: What do these items tell me about this person? What might they care about? This gives you a starting point for conversation that is rooted in observation rather than pre-planned talking points.

⇒ **Notice Clothing and Accessories:** People often express their personalities, interests, and values through the clothes they wear or the accessories they choose. If someone is wearing a jacket with a sports team logo, a distinctive piece of jewelry, or a lapel pin, those are all clues you can use to start a conversation. For instance, "I noticed the [team] logo on your jacket—are you a big fan?"

⇒ **Be Curious, Not Nosy:** When you use observation to start a conversation, approach it with curiosity, not prying. The goal isn't to interrogate the person or make them uncomfortable but to create a sense of ease and engagement. For example, if you notice a photo from a vacation, you might say, "That looks like an amazing place—where you were when this was taken." rather than, "Where do you travel on vacation?" The former shows interest without feeling intrusive, while the latter could feel more like a personal probe.

⇒ **Watch for Emotional Cues:** Beyond physical objects, you can also observe emotional cues in someone's demeanor. Are they smiling or fidgeting? Does their body language suggest they're excited or anxious? These observations allow you to adjust your tone or the direction of the conversation accordingly. If someone seems a bit tense, you might ease into the conversation with a light observation about their environment to help them relax.

Why This Works: The Psychology of Being Seen

There's a deep psychological principle at play when you use observation to begin a conversation: *People want to be seen*. We all have a need to be acknowledged and validated. When someone takes the time to notice something unique about us—whether it's our interests, our achievements, or even just the way we've arranged our space—it feels good. It's a subtle way of saying, "You matter."

By beginning a conversation based on observation, you're giving the other person a gift: the chance to share something personal in a natural, unforced way. You're telling them, "I see you, and I'm interested in you." This creates an immediate connection, making it more likely that the conversation will flow naturally and move into deeper, more meaningful territory.

Tell Me . . .

Conversations Born from Curiosity

At its core, observation is about curiosity. Great conversationalists are naturally curious about the world around them. They don't just look—they *see*. They don't just hear—they *listen*. They notice the details that others might miss, and they use those details to fuel their interactions. When you approach conversations with a mindset of curiosity, you open yourself up to learning something new about the other person.

Curiosity-driven conversations are also more engaging because they're personal. Instead of relying on generic questions like, "What do you do for a living?" you can ask something specific and unexpected. This not only makes the conversation more interesting but also sets you apart as someone who is genuinely invested in connecting with others.

Observation in Action

Let's put this into practice. Suppose you're at a networking event and you're about to introduce yourself to someone new. Instead of jumping straight into the usual small talk, take a moment to observe. What are they wearing? Is there something distinctive about their shoes or tie? Do they have a name tag with a company you're familiar with? Use that observation to kick off the conversation.

You might say, "I couldn't help but notice the company logo on your badge—I've always been interested in what you all do." Or if they're holding a book, you could ask, "I see you've got *[book title]* with you: Tell me your favorite part so far." These are small but meaningful ways to break the ice.

Observation, Conversation, and Serendipity

During a business trip to Paris, a friend and I decided to carve out a day for something uniquely French: a visit to Épernay, the birthplace of Champagne and home to the renowned Moët & Chandon winery. A smooth trip there by train was in the plans, but fate had other ideas. Midway through, our train made an unexpected stop in Meaux, a commune about 40 kilometers from Paris, stranding us at the station for two hours while a mechanical issue was sorted out. With time on our hands and no place to go, we settled in to wait, shrugging off our original itinerary.

As we stood there, taking in the surroundings of the station, I noticed two Americans nearby, chatting and looking just as stuck as we were. With nothing to lose, I walked over, introduced myself and struck up a conversation. Soon I learned they were James and Evan, food and beverage directors for two major Atlantic City casinos. Small world—it turned out they were also headed to Épernay, with a personalized tour scheduled at Moët & Chandon that had been set up by their casino's wine supplier. They mentioned that they'd be more than happy for us to join them, a rare and unexpected invitation we enthusiastically accepted.

When we finally arrived, we were welcomed by Henri Perrier, a tall, impeccably dressed French gentleman with an air of distinction you couldn't miss. He guided us through a private tour of the Moët & Chandon caves, leading us through vaulted chambers lined with bottles that seemed to hold the secrets of centuries past. As if the experience wasn't already extraordinary, Henri gifted each of us with bottles of Dom Pérignon to take home.

Our luck only continued to build from there. Because of our delayed arrival, Henri invited us to join a small group of restaurateurs from Paris for a private seven-course lunch, each course accompanied by a carefully selected Champagne or wine that elevated every bite. The meal was unforgettable, a true sensory journey that effortlessly combined food and drink into something magical.

Tell Me . . .

Following lunch, Henri led us to an intimate parlor where we were served Cognac, café, and Cuban cigars, rounding off our day in classic French style. We lingered, deep in conversation and laughter with new-found friends, savoring the final notes of an experience that was as rare as it was serendipitous.

Looking back, I'm convinced it was that simple conversation at the station that made this unforgettable day possible. I am also convinced that if we'd had smartphones back then, we would have been texting and scrolling and would have never engaged James and Evan, now friends, in conversation. Striking up a dialogue with two strangers brought us not just an invitation, but an opportunity to connect, to experience, and to savor a day that I doubt could ever be replicated. Sometimes, the best opportunities come not from the plans we make, but from the chance encounters along the way.

At first glance, observation might seem like a simple or even superficial tool for starting conversations. But its power lies in the fact that it makes the other person feel seen. By noticing and commenting on the details of their world, you're showing that you care about more than just the surface-level exchange of words. You're interested in the person behind the conversation.

So, the next time you're about to engage someone in conversation, take a moment to observe. Look around. Notice the details. Then, use those observations as the bridge to a deeper, more meaningful exchange. Who knows, you might just find yourself enjoying one of the more memorable experiences of your life.

Pause and Ponder: Take a minute or two to think about random and memorable encounters you have had with interesting people. Think about what might have been lost if, in the moments leading up to the encounter, you would have been aimlessly scrolling your social media feed.

Tell Me . . .

Key Takeaways from Chapter 13

- ⇒ Observation is a powerful tool for initiating authentic and engaging conversations.
- ⇒ Noticing small details about a person or their environment allows you to focus on them rather than yourself, creating a deeper connection.
- ⇒ Simple observations—like a photo, an award, or an accessory—can spark meaningful discussions that move beyond surface-level small talk.
- ⇒ Developing your observational skills requires practice and curiosity, but it opens doors to richer, more personal exchanges.
- ⇒ Conversations rooted in observation often lead to unexpected and memorable experiences, as illustrated by the story of serendipity at the Champagne winery.
- ⇒ Tell me YOUR key takeaway:

_____

Action Item

Before your next interaction, pause and observe your surroundings. Notice a single detail about the person or environment and use it to spark a meaningful conversation. Let curiosity guide you to deeper connections.

"You can have everything in life you want if you will just help enough other people get what they want."

—*Zig Ziglar*

Chapter 14

The Value of Showing Interest In Others

We live in a world increasingly dominated by distractions and surface-level interactions, a world that fosters disconnection. One of the most powerful ways to connect with someone is also the simplest: *showing genuine interest*. When you take the time to truly engage with another person—listening to their story, asking about their experiences, or even just noticing the details of their life—you communicate something deeper than mere politeness. You tell them, "You matter." They no longer feel invisible; they are seen.

The value of showing interest in others goes beyond making conversation. It builds trust, fosters mutual respect, and creates lasting relationships—whether in personal, social, or professional settings. In this chapter, we'll explore how showing interest in others can transform the quality of your interactions, turning routine exchanges into meaningful connections others can transform the quality of your interactions, turning routine exchanges into meaningful connections.

Tell Me . . .

The Psychology Behind Feeling Valued

At the heart of every conversation lies a fundamental human need: the need to feel valued. Psychologists have long understood that one of the most powerful drivers of human behavior is the desire for connection and validation. We want to be seen, heard, and understood. When someone takes an interest in us—whether by asking questions, listening attentively, or showing curiosity about our lives (or our work)—we feel that we matter.

This is why showing genuine interest in others can be so transformative. It satisfies that deep-seated need for validation, making the other person feel appreciated and respected. And when people feel valued, they're more likely to open up, trust you, and engage in a more authentic way.

Consider the difference between two types of conversations. In one, someone asks you, "How are you?" but doesn't listen to the answer. They move on quickly, their mind clearly elsewhere. In the other, someone asks the same question but follows up with, "Really? Tell me more." They listen, respond thoughtfully, and show that they genuinely care about your answer. Which conversation makes you feel seen? Which makes you feel valued?

When you show interest in others, you're not just engaging in polite conversation. You're fulfilling a universal human need for connection. After all, we are social creatures.

The Power of Asking Questions

One of the simplest and most effective ways to show interest in others is by asking questions. But not just any questions—*thoughtful, open-ended questions* that invite people to share more about themselves. The opener, of course, is not a question at all. The phrase "Tell Me . . ." is the perfect entry point into this kind of conversation. It signals that you're not just looking for a quick answer—you're inviting the other person to share their story, their thoughts, and their experiences.

Consider how a simple shift in phrasing can change the tone of a conversation:

- ⇒ Instead of asking, "Did you have a good weekend?" try asking, "Tell me about the highlight of your weekend."
- ⇒ Instead of asking, "Do you like your job?" try asking, "Tell me what you enjoy most about your work."
- ⇒ Instead of asking, "How was the trip?" try asking, "Tell me about the best part of your trip."

These kinds of questions do more than just elicit information—they invite the other person to open up. They create a sense of curiosity and engagement, showing that you're genuinely interested in what they have to say. And when people feel that someone is truly listening, they're more likely to share not just the surface-level facts but also the emotions, thoughts, and experiences that lie beneath.

An Unexpected Friendship: How Showing Interest Can Open Doors

A few years ago, a colleague of mine, David, found himself at a networking event that, by all accounts, seemed unremarkable. It was a routine corporate mixer, filled with the usual suspects: executives in suits, a buzz of surface-level conversation, and the polite exchange of business cards. But amidst the crowd, David noticed someone who didn't seem to quite fit in—a man dressed in worn-out clothes, standing quietly in the corner.

Most people at the event didn't pay him any attention, assuming he wasn't part of their world. But David was curious. He approached the man, introduced himself, and asked, "Tell me what brings you here tonight." The man seemed taken aback by the interest but responded by explaining that

Tell Me . . .

he was a groundskeeper for the venue and had simply wandered into the event after finishing his shift.

Instead of brushing him off, David asked more questions. "Tell me about your job and what you enjoy most about it." The man, who had likely been overlooked by nearly everyone at the event, began to open up. He shared stories about his work, the pride he took in maintaining the gardens, and how he had learned the trade from his father. As they spoke, David learned that the man also had a small landscaping business on the side.

They exchanged contact information, and over the next few months, David and the groundskeeper struck up an unlikely friendship. David ended up hiring him to landscape his own property, and through word of mouth, the man's business began to grow. What started as a simple conversation—driven by curiosity and a willingness to show interest in someone others had ignored—turned into a rewarding relationship for both parties.

This story is a reminder that you never know where showing genuine interest in someone can lead. By looking past superficial differences and engaging with others as human beings, you open the door to connections you might otherwise miss.

Listening with Purpose

As we discussed in chapter 11, asking great questions is only half the equation. The other half is *listening with purpose*. It's not enough to simply ask questions and then move on to the next topic. You must be fully present, engaged, and responsive to what the other person is saying.

Active listening is an art, and it requires more than just hearing words. It involves listening to tone, picking up on subtle cues, and reflecting on what the other person has said. It's about making the conversation a two-way street, where the speaker feels heard and the listener shows understanding.

One way to demonstrate this kind of listening is through acknowledgment and follow-up questions. When someone shares a story or thought, acknowledge what they've said before moving forward. For example:

⇒ "That's really interesting—tell me when that happened."
⇒ "I didn't realize you were involved in that project. Tell me more about your role."
⇒ "Wow, that sounds like a major challenge. Tell me how you handled it."

These kinds of responses show that you're not just waiting for your turn to speak—you're actively engaged in the conversation. You're showing interest not just by asking questions but by digging deeper into the other person's experiences.

The Ripple Effect of Genuine Interest

Showing interest in others doesn't just benefit the person you're talking to—it has a ripple effect that extends beyond the conversation. When you make someone feel valued, they're more likely to value the relationship as well. This creates a sense of mutual respect and reciprocity that can lead to stronger, more meaningful connections.

Think about it: When someone shows genuine interest in your life, how does it make you feel? More than likely, it makes you want to invest in the relationship, to engage more deeply, and to reciprocate that interest. The same is true in reverse. When you show interest in others, you're laying the foundation for a relationship built on mutual appreciation.

This ripple effect is especially powerful in professional settings. In business, showing interest in others is one of the most effective ways to build trust, foster collaboration, and create opportunities for future partnerships. People want to work with those who listen to and care about their ideas, challenges, and goals. Whether you're in a meeting with colleagues, engaging with clients, or networking with potential partners, taking the time to show genuine interest can set you apart and create lasting connections.

The Empathy Connection

At its core, showing interest in others is about *empathy*. It's about stepping outside of your own perspective and engaging with someone else's world. Empathy is one of the most powerful tools we have for building relationships because it allows us to understand, validate, and connect with the emotions of others.

When you show interest in someone's experiences—whether it's their work, their family, their hobbies, or their challenges—you're practicing empathy. You're saying, "I want to understand what you're going through. I care about your perspective." This kind of empathetic engagement makes people feel seen and valued on a deeper level, which strengthens the connection between you.

Empathy doesn't just improve individual conversations—it can transform the entire dynamic of a relationship. When people feel understood, they're more likely to be open, honest, and trusting. In both personal and professional settings, this leads to stronger, more authentic connections.

The Long-Term Impact

The value of showing interest in others extends far beyond the initial conversation. The connections you build by being genuinely curious and engaged can last for years, if not a lifetime. People remember those who took the time to listen to them, who asked thoughtful questions, and who made them feel valued.

This long-term impact is especially important in professional settings. Whether you're leading a team, building a business, or simply networking, the relationships you cultivate through genuine interest are the ones that will last. People want to work with, follow, and support those who have made them feel important and understood.

In your personal life, showing interest in others deepens relationships and creates lasting bonds. Whether it's with friends, family, or your spouse, taking the time to be curious about their experiences strengthens the emotional connection between you. It shows that you're invested in their happiness, success, and well-being.

Here are some ways you can show interest in others:

- ⇒ **Ask Open-Ended Prompts**: Start with "Tell Me..." or other open-ended statements that invite the other person to share more about their experiences, thoughts, or feelings.
- ⇒ **Listen Actively**: Be fully present in the conversation. Don't think about what you're going to say next. Focus on what the other person is saying and respond thoughtfully.
- ⇒ **Follow Up**: Don't just ask a question and move on. Ask follow-up questions that show you're genuinely interested in learning more.
- ⇒ **Acknowledge What's Shared**: Reflect on what the person has shared. Acknowledge their experiences and emotions before diving into the next topic.
- ⇒ **Practice Empathy**: Try to understand the other person's perspective. Put yourself in their shoes and respond with empathy and compassion.

The Simple Power of Showing Interest

The value of showing interest in others cannot be overstated. It's one of the simplest yet most powerful ways to build deeper connections, foster

Tell Me . . .

trust, and create lasting relationships. Whether you're in a professional setting or spending time with loved ones, showing genuine curiosity about the people around you can transform the quality of your interactions. It's not just about having better conversations—it's about building a life filled with richer, more meaningful relationships.

Key Takeaways from Chapter 14

⇒ Genuinely engage with others by listening attentively and asking thoughtful questions.
⇒ People have an innate need to feel valued and heard.
⇒ Starting with open-ended questions, such as "Tell me . . . ," invites others to share more about their experiences, promoting deeper engagement.
⇒ Listening with purpose is essential—engage fully, reflect on what's shared, and ask follow-up questions to deepen understanding.
⇒ Showing interest not only strengthens individual relationships but also fosters reciprocity, which enhances both personal and professional networks.
⇒ Practicing empathy by seeking to understand others' perspectives enhances trust.
⇒ Tell me YOUR key takeaway:

_____

Action Item

Start conversations with open-ended prompts like "Tell me about your experience with . . . ," and actively listen to the answers, showing curiosity and empathy with follow-up questions to deepen your engagement and connection.

Part 4

Putting It All To Work

"People become the stories they hear and the stories they tell."

— *Elie Wiesel*

Chapter 15

Storytelling

The Stories Within You

Conversation is not just a one-way street wherein you just listen and nod. There are times when you will have to step into the space to make a significant contribution to the discussion. Storytelling is an ideal way to do that.

Whether or not you realize it, you have an abundance of stories within you—stories that are begging to be told. They exist in your experiences, relationships, and daily interactions, often lying dormant, waiting for the right moment to surface. Each conversation, challenge, and success you experience carries within it a narrative thread that, when woven together, creates the rich tapestry of your life. And while you may not always recognize the value of these stories, they have the potential to inspire, connect, and transform.

Storytelling is not reserved for great writers or charismatic speakers. It is a natural part of being human. From the stories we tell ourselves about our lives to the tales we share with others over dinner, the act of storytelling is a fundamental way we make sense of the world. Everyone, regardless of background or experience, has a unique perspective worth sharing. The challenge lies in embracing the storyteller within and learning how to bring these narratives to life with authenticity and purpose.

In this chapter, we will explore the art of storytelling and uncover how you can tap into the wealth of stories within you. Whether you're leading a meeting, giving a presentation, or simply engaging in a heartfelt conversation, storytelling can elevate the way you communicate and connect with others. Let's begin by discovering the hidden gems of your own life and transforming them into compelling narratives that leave a lasting impact.

Personal Reflection

Born into a family of Lebanese immigrants, I grew up in a vibrant household where storytelling was more than a tradition; it was a way of life. In my family, stories were told with such vividness and passion that they became the fabric of everyday existence. Each family member, without exception, was a natural storyteller who could captivate an audience, large or small, with their tales. They didn't just tell stories; they embodied them, using animated body language, expressive gestures, and varied vocal inflections and accents to bring their narratives to life. They *became* the story. This immersive environment instilled in me a profound appreciation for the art of conversation and a deep understanding of its power to connect, influence, and inspire.

My early exposure to the rich tapestry of my family's storytelling traditions laid the foundation for a lifelong commitment to mastering and teaching communication as a crafted art form. As a young boy, I watched my relatives engage effortlessly with people from all walks of life, never shying away from an opportunity to connect, share, learn, and entertain. I observed how these interactions built bridges, fostered understanding, and created bonds that could withstand the test of time. Inspired by this, it became my mission to become a skilled conversationalist and to share this gift with others.

> **Pause and Ponder:** Think about your exposure to storytelling when you were growing up. Who were the standout storytellers in your family? What made them and their stories stand out? Do you channel them when you tell stories yourself? How do others respond or react to your stories? What is one thing you could do to improve your skills as a storyteller?

The Universal Thread: How Stories Connect Us All

Stories are the threads that bind us. They are the echoes of our past, the bridges to our future, and the glue that holds our relationships together. Storytelling, the art of crafting and sharing these narratives, transcends cultures and ages. It's not just about entertainment; it's a primal and fundamental human tool with profound impacts on business, social interaction, and family life.

In the realm of business, storytelling is no longer a mere marketing gimmick. It's a strategic advantage. Facts and figures *tell*, but stories *sell*. A compelling narrative about a company's origin, its mission, or the impact of its products can resonate far deeper with customers than a dry list of features. Take Patagonia, for example. The outdoor apparel company weaves stories of environmental activism and adventure into its marketing, fostering a sense of community and shared values with its audience.

Stories can also be used to build trust and loyalty. Imagine a business presentation that goes beyond dry statistics and instead presents a customer's success story. This narrative approach taps into human empathy, allowing potential clients to envision themselves experiencing similar positive outcomes. Additionally, stories can foster a strong internal company culture. Sharing the struggles and triumphs of past endeavors can inspire employees, create a sense of shared purpose, and motivate them to contribute to the company's narrative.

When we step outside the boardroom, storytelling plays a crucial role in social settings. It's the lifeblood of conversation, the tool we use to connect with others. Sharing a funny anecdote about a recent trip or a heartwarming tale from your childhood can spark laughter, empathy, and a sense of camaraderie. Stories allow us to share experiences, even if they're vastly different, by creating a bridge of understanding.

Furthermore, stories can be powerful instruments for social change. Consider movements like Black Lives Matter or #MeToo. These movements rely heavily on storytelling to raise awareness, generate empathy, and galvanize public support. By sharing personal experiences of injustice, these movements not only raise awareness but also create a sense of shared struggle, fostering solidarity and inspiring action.

Within the intimate space of family life, storytelling plays an even more profound role. Sharing stories about family history and traditions creates a sense of belonging and identity for children. It is about roots. Hearing tales of their grandparents' triumphs and struggles allows them to connect with their past and understand their place in the family lineage. Storytelling also fosters strong emotional bonds. Sharing bedtime stories or recounting the day's events creates a space for connection, allowing families to express love, share values, and build lasting memories.

The power of storytelling doesn't diminish with age. Grandparents, for example, can pass down their wisdom and life lessons by weaving stories of their experiences. This not only entertains younger generations but also strengthens familial ties and preserves cultural heritage.

However, it's important to remember that storytelling comes with a responsibility. Stories can be used to manipulate or mislead. When crafting narratives, it's crucial to strive for authenticity, transparency, and integrity.

Thoughtful Use of Humor in Storytelling

Humor, when used intentionally and appropriately, is a powerful tool in storytelling. It breaks the ice, lightens the mood, and creates an immediate sense of connection between the storyteller and the audience. A well-timed, lighthearted remark can make a message more engaging, memorable, and even persuasive.

In a business setting, a touch of self-deprecating humor can make you more approachable and relatable, helping to build trust with clients or colleagues. At family gatherings, shared laughter strengthens bonds and makes stories more vivid and enjoyable.

However, the key to using humor effectively is mindfulness. Consider the context, the audience, and the potential impact of your words. Avoid humor that might alienate, offend, or distract from your message. Instead, aim for inclusive, uplifting humor that enhances your story rather than overshadowing its purpose. Attending a seminar delivered by the notable motivational speaker, Zig Ziglar, I recall him referring to the use of off-color language and humor and saying, "You can never rise above your words." The spoken word can easily create a negative impression that could be challenging to overcome.

Used thoughtfully, humor can be the element that transforms a simple story into an unforgettable experience.

Tell Me . . .

Impact of Imagination

Storytelling is an inherent human capacity with far-reaching impact. To be a good storyteller, you must *be* the story. It is important you embrace and emulate the characters, become animated and create a visual of the moments.

From boardrooms to dinner tables, stories have the power to connect, inspire, and build a stronger sense of community. By harnessing the impact of narrative, we can strengthen our businesses, social bonds, and families and create a more empathetic and connected world.

Effective storytelling can be the secret weapon that closes deals. Facts and figures are important but can leave customers feeling cold and detached. A well-crafted story, however, taps into emotions and creates a connection. Imagine a salesperson sharing a story about a client with similar challenges who saw significant improvement after using their product. This narrative allows potential customers to envision themselves experiencing the same success, fostering trust and a sense of urgency to secure the same positive outcome. Stories can paint a vivid picture of the problem your product or service solves, the ideal future it creates, and the clear path your company offers to get them there. By weaving a compelling narrative, you can move customers from simple awareness to enthusiastic action.

Guilty or Not Guilty

In the movie *A Time to Kill*, a fictional courtroom drama based upon John Grisham's best-selling book, Matthew McConaughey portrays Jake Brigance, a young attorney tasked with defending Carl Lee Hailey, a Black man accused of killing two white men to avenge the assault they perpetrated on his ten-year-old daughter. Taking place in the racially charged Deep South, the case seems unwinnable, the odds stacked against him in a community divided by prejudice. But it is Jake's closing argument—an unforgettable, masterfully crafted piece of storytelling—that turns the tide.

With the jury hanging on his every word, Jake begins by painting a vivid and heart-wrenching picture of the tragedy that befell Carl Lee's young daughter. He invites the jurors to close their eyes and imagine the horrific scene, describing it in painstaking detail that evokes deep emotions. His voice wavers with the weight of the injustice, and his words drip with empathy and urgency. Jake doesn't simply recount the facts—he makes the jury feel the terror, heartbreak, and anger as if they were living it themselves.

In a final, gut-wrenching twist, Jake pauses for a moment then asks the jury to imagine that the young victim is *white*. The room falls silent, the unspoken realities of racism laid bare. The simplicity and raw honesty of his narrative cut through years of ingrained prejudice, forcing the jury to confront the humanity of the Hailey family.

Carl Lee Hailey was found "not guilty."

__Disclaimer:__ This is a fictional story, intended only as an illustration of the power of storytelling. Jake's ability to draw the jury into an empathetic experience demonstrates how a well-told story can transcend barriers, open minds, and ignite change, even in the face of impossible odds.

Memorable and Repeatable

There are two critical characteristics which can transform an ordinary narrative into an impactful and enduring experience: The story must be *memorable* and *repeatable*. Otherwise, what is the purpose of telling a story?

⇒ **Memorable:** A story becomes memorable when it resonates deeply with its audience, leaving a lasting impression. This is achieved through vivid imagery, compelling characters, and emotional connections. When a story is memorable, it sticks with the listener long after it has been told, influencing thoughts, feelings, and behaviors. A memorable story often includes unique details, relatable experiences, or profound insights that evoke emotions, making the story personal and impactful. Whether through humor, drama, or inspiration, these stories stay with people, becoming a part of their internal dialogue and shaping their perspectives.

⇒ **Repeatable:** A repeatable story is one that can be easily shared and retold by others, spreading its influence beyond the initial audience. For a story to be repeatable, it must be clear, concise, and structured in a way that makes it easy to recall and convey. Repeatable stories often contain simple yet powerful messages or morals that are universally understood. The more a story is repeated, the more it reinforces its lessons and values, creating a ripple effect that extends its reach and impact.

In effective storytelling, the interplay between "memorable" and "repeatable" elements ensures that stories not only capture attention but also sustain it, allowing them to be passed along, remembered, and cherished over time.

Memorable and Repeatable in Seven Words

In high-stakes situations, the difference between persuading and failing often hinges on saying something memorable and repeatable. Johnny Cochran's closing argument in the O. J. Simpson trial is a classic example of how powerful a well-crafted, unforgettable line can be.

The year was 1995, and the courtroom was tense with the weight of a case that had captured global attention. In the culmination of months of testimony, legal arguments, and a media frenzy, Cochran knew he needed a line that would stick in the minds of the jurors long after they left the courtroom. As he approached the jury box, he delivered the line that would define the case, and perhaps his career: "If it doesn't fit, you must acquit." This simple rhyme captured a core element of the defense: the infamous glove, which appeared not to fit Simpson when he tried it on in front of the jury. With those words, Cochran created a lasting image that would echo in the minds of jurors.

In the deliberation room, that phrase likely became a rallying cry among those leaning toward acquittal. Jurors might have found themselves repeating it to reinforce their reasoning or to persuade others. Instead of recalling the mounds of complex evidence, they only needed to hold on to that one rhythmic line. It was simple, clear, and irrefutable in its message. The line helped shift the focus away from intricate forensic details to a tangible, visual moment they'd all witnessed together.

Ultimately, the jury returned with a "not guilty" verdict, and Cochran's line was immortalized as a masterstroke in courtroom rhetoric. This case highlights a critical lesson: If you want to win people over, your message must be memorable and repeatable. Whether in a courtroom, a boardroom, or even a casual conversation, finding a way to make your point stick can mean the difference between success and failure. Cochran's line wasn't just clever—it was strategic. By making it easy to remember and hard to dismiss, he gave the jury a tool they could use to sway opinion. In Cochran's words, delivered with rhythm and clarity, he left a lasting impact, showing the persuasive power of being memorable and repeatable.

The Story Closed the Deal

As I stepped into the sleek, modern office of a potential client, a pang of nostalgia washed over me. The polished wooden desk, the scent of leather chairs, and the soft glow of antique lamps instantly reminded me of my father's office from my childhood. In that moment, I decided to open the meeting in a way that felt authentic and personal.

"Your office reminds me of my father's office," I said, my voice reminiscent. "Before we begin, may I share a brief personal story about one of my fondest memories in that office as a little boy?"

Mr. Anderson, the prospect, leaned forward with interest and a soft smile. "Of course, please do," he replied, intrigued by the unexpected turn of conversation.

Smiling, I recounted a cherished memory of spending weekends with my father in his office, sitting together amidst stacks of paperwork, sharing stories and laughter. As I spoke, I noticed Mr. Anderson's expression soften, and he nodded in understanding.

"That's a beautiful memory," he said, his eyes reflecting a hint of nostalgia. "It reminds me of my own father's office."

And just like that, a connection formed between us, built upon shared experiences and cherished moments with our fathers. Mr. Anderson went on to share his own story of visiting his father's office as a child, painting a vivid picture of a time long gone but deeply treasured.

As the meeting progressed, the atmosphere shifted from formal to familiar. By the time I presented my proposal, there was a sense of camaraderie and understanding between us. In the end, it wasn't just about the product or the deal—it was about the genuine connection we had established through storytelling. And as we shook hands, I knew this was more than just a business transaction—it was the beginning of a meaningful partnership, grounded in shared memories and mutual respect.

Our professional and personal relationship continued until Mr. Anderson's passing eleven years later.

Key Takeaways from Chapter 15

⇒ Your personal experiences, challenges, and relationships contain stories that can connect, inspire, and transform.
⇒ Storytelling is not limited to professionals or great speakers. Everyone is a storyteller, and embracing this skill can enhance communication in any environment.
⇒ Stories resonate more than facts. They tap into emotions, empathy, and shared human experiences, helping to build trust and influence decisions.
⇒ A good story sticks with the audience and can be easily retold. A memorable, repeatable narrative can inspire action and make a lasting impact.
⇒ Tell me YOUR key takeaway:

_____

Action Item

Embrace storytelling in your everyday interactions. Whether in meetings, casual conversations, or presentations, start weaving personal stories into your communication. Reflect on your own experiences and think about how they might connect with others' values and emotions. Focus on authenticity and clarity, aiming to make your story both memorable and repeatable.

"If time be of all things the most precious, wasting time must be the greatest prodigality."

—*Benjamin Franklin*

Chapter 16

Time Kills Deals

There was a small plaque on his desk. It read, "Time Kills Deals." It sat there unobtrusively, just a few words on a polished brass surface. But it represented something far larger than a clever phrase; it embodied a worldview, a deep understanding of how the world of business—and, more broadly, human relationships—operates.

My uncle, Edmund Reggie, was a lawyer, but not just any lawyer. He was a dealmaker, a politico, a power broker, someone who thrived in the high-stakes, high-pressure environment where deals were struck or undone in the blink of an eye. For him, *time* wasn't an abstract concept. It was a tangible, ever-present force. Every moment that passed was an opportunity gained or lost, a chance to move forward or stall. He understood this better than most, and it shaped the way he worked, the way he built relationships, and the way he closed deals. He also respected the value of time when working to help family and friends, always responding to requests without hesitation. It was just who he was.

At its core, the idea that *time kills deals* is deceptively simple. It speaks to the urgency of action and response. Yet, as we'll explore, it touches on something profound about how we interact with one another in business

Tell Me . . .

and in life. It's a principle that operates in the background, unseen but potent, driving behavior in ways we rarely stop to consider.

The Nature of Time

Let's begin with a simple observation: Time is *not* neutral. This isn't just true in physics, where Einstein's theory of relativity teaches us that time warps and bends. It's true in everyday life, particularly in the world of business.

We tend to think of time as a passive element in our transactions and relationships. When we receive an email from a client or a colleague, we may set it aside for later, assuming that nothing will change between now and when we respond. But this assumption is flawed. Time is not a blank space between actions—it's an active participant in every interaction we have.

What Edmund understood, and what too many of us fail to grasp, is that *waiting* is not a neutral state. It's a state of decay. The longer you wait to respond to a client's inquiry or an opportunity, the more the chances of success erode. Doubts grow. Uncertainty creeps in. Trust, once solid, begins to weaken.

This phenomenon plays out across industries. A prospective buyer emails a real estate agent, expressing interest in a property. Hours pass, then a day, then two. Each hour of silence chips away at the buyer's enthusiasm. By the time the agent finally responds, the buyer may have moved on—physically to another property, mentally to another agent, emotionally to another idea. The deal is dead, not because the property wasn't right or the price wasn't fair, but because time did what it always does: It filled the empty space with doubt and distraction.

The Power of Swift Action

In contrast to the corrosive effects of time, consider the impact of a rapid response. When someone reaches out to you and receives an immediate reply, something magical happens. Trust is established. Momentum builds. The client feels seen and valued, and suddenly the deal feels possible, even inevitable.

Edmund was a master of this. He made it a rule to respond to every inquiry, every client communication, within hours—sometimes within minutes. Even if he didn't have the full answer yet, he would acknowledge the communication, signaling that he was on it, that their concern or opportunity mattered to him.

This wasn't just a courtesy; it was an engrained belief. He knew that quick action kept deals alive, kept clients engaged, kept the momentum going. And in the business world, momentum is everything. It's what turns ideas into reality, conversations into contracts, and prospects into partnerships.

This isn't merely a business strategy. It's a fundamental truth about human interaction. When someone responds quickly, we feel important. When they delay, we feel neglected. It's as true in personal relationships as it is in professional ones. Time has the same effect on a potential deal as it does on a friendship or a romantic relationship: It either nourishes it or erodes it.

Ghosting: The Silent Deal Killer

If time kills deals, then ghosting—the act of disappearing, of failing to respond—is the ultimate deal killer.

Ghosting, a term popularized in the world of dating, has unfortunately become all too common in business as well. You send an email, leave a voicemail, follow up again—and hear nothing. Days pass. Weeks. The silence becomes deafening.

In business, ghosting isn't just unprofessional; it's destructive. The absence of a response leaves the other party in a state of limbo. Are they still interested? Should I wait, or should I move on? And each day of silence breeds more frustration, more uncertainty. Deals die not because of active rejection but because of passive inaction.

Why do people ghost? It's rarely malicious. More often than not, it's a combination of avoidance, overwhelm, and indecision. The person on the other end doesn't know how to respond, so they don't. They don't want to give bad news, so they avoid giving any news. They're too busy, so they put it off until tomorrow, and then tomorrow becomes next week.

But the effect is always the same. The silence speaks volumes. And once a client feels ghosted, it's nearly impossible to regain their trust.

The Simple Act of Picking Up the Phone

Email, texts, and Slack messages dominate the landscape of communication today. It is no wonder we've forgotten the power of direct communication. But there's an elegant simplicity in picking up the phone or, better yet, walking into someone's office and saying, "Tell me..."

This was another of my uncle's core beliefs. When a deal was stalling or a client seemed uncertain, he wouldn't rely on email chains or a long-winded back-and-forth. He would make a call. He would sit down with them. And he would start with two words: "Tell me..."

Why is this so effective? Because it opens the door to conversation. It invites the other person to explain what's on their mind. It turns a potentially confrontational moment into a collaborative one. It brings humanity into the situation.

"Tell me what's going on."
"Tell me what's holding things up."
"Tell me what you need to feel comfortable moving forward."

This simple phrase diffuses tension and brings clarity. It's a way of cutting through the fog of uncertainty and hesitation. It's a way of saying, "I'm here, I'm listening, and I want to keep this moving."

The Cost of Hesitation

If ghosting is the silent killer of deals, hesitation is its close cousin. We hesitate for all sorts of reasons: We're unsure of the right decision, we're afraid of making a mistake, or we simply don't know what to say. But in business, hesitation is often more dangerous than making the wrong move.

Deals, like any dynamic system, require momentum. Without it, they stall. The longer you wait to act, the harder it becomes to regain that momentum. Opportunities slip away, and by the time you're ready to act, it's too late.

My uncle understood this intuitively. He didn't believe in rushing decisions, but he also knew that waiting too long to act was just as risky. His motto was always, *Keep things moving forward.* Even if you don't have all the answers, even if you're unsure of the next step, act. Because in the world of deals, as in life, the cost of inaction is often far greater than the cost of a misstep.

Time Kills Deals. It's a deceptively simple phrase, but it captures something fundamental about how we operate in business and in life. Time is not neutral. It's either working for you or against you. It's either building momentum or eroding trust. And if you're not careful, time will quietly, inevitably, kill *your* deals.

Tell Me . . .

So, act. Respond quickly. Pick up the phone. Say "Tell me . . ." Keep things moving forward. Because in the end, it's not time that kills deals. It's our failure to recognize how powerful time really is.

> **Pause and Ponder:** Have you ever been ghosted? How did you feel? Have you ever ghosted someone, waiting more than 48 hours to respond to their call, email, or text? What kept you from responding in a timelier fashion? Beginning today, what will you do to ensure you never ghost anyone again?

Key Takeaways from Chapter 16

⇒ Time is not neutral. Time is an active participant in business and relationships.
⇒ Swift action builds momentum. It keeps deals alive and prevents stagnation.
⇒ Ghosting is destructive and is the silent deal killer.
⇒ The power of direct communication and personal interaction, like phone calls, fosters trust and clarity.
⇒ Waiting too long to act, even out of uncertainty, can destroy momentum.
⇒ Tell me YOUR key takeaway:

_____

Action Item

When an opportunity arises (one certainly will within the next twenty-four hours) or a client reaches out, act within *five seconds*. Whether it's sending an acknowledgment or making a quick phone call, moving quickly maintains momentum and prevents doubt from setting in. This is particularly critical if you anticipate receiving or having to deliver less-than-pleasant news. Respond quickly.

> "If I interview someone for an hour, I'm looking for four amazing minutes."
>
> —*Claudio Fernández-Aráoz*

Chapter 17

Interviews: A Win-Win Approach

When we think of interviews, we often picture a structured back-and-forth—questions carefully crafted to extract key information.

"Why do you want this job?"
"What are your strengths?"
"Why are you leaving?"

These questions are designed to evaluate, to measure, to categorize. But what if the best interviews weren't about questions at all? What if, instead of interrogating, we simply invited people to share?

That's where "Tell Me . . ." changes everything.

Two simple words. Yet within them lies the potential for transformation. Unlike standard interview questions that prompt rehearsed responses, "Tell Me . . ." invites honesty, depth, and authenticity. For the interviewer, it reveals insights that scripted answers never could. For the interviewee, it creates an opportunity to share their story, their motivations, and their true character.

By shifting from interrogation to conversation, we turn interviews into powerful, mutually beneficial exchanges. Whether it's a job interview, a

Tell Me . . .

college interview, an exit interview, or a performance review, "Tell Me . . ." fosters trust, deepens understanding, and leads to decisions based on real human connection.

But "Tell Me . . ." isn't just for interviewers. Interviewees can use it too. By flipping the script and inviting the interviewer to share, candidates can create a richer, more engaging dialogue—one that leaves a lasting impression.

Let's explore how this simple phrase benefits both sides in different interview settings.

Job Interviews: Beyond the Resume
For the Interviewer: Gain Authentic Insights

Traditional interview questions often produce well-rehearsed answers.

"Why do you want this job?" might yield a polished response about alignment with company values. But does it reveal true motivation? Instead, try:

"Tell me what drew you to this company." "Tell me about a time when your team truly made an impact."

"Tell me about a challenge this role will help solve."

Watch as the candidate pauses, stepping away from their script. Instead of a generic answer, they may share a personal experience with the brand, an influential mentor, or a pivotal moment in their career. You won't just learn what they think—you'll learn what they feel. And those feelings often reveal true passion and cultural fit.

For the Interviewee: Stand Out by Engaging in Dialogue

Most candidates prepare to check boxes—experience, skills, qualifications. But when invited to tell their story, they can highlight their

personal journey, the obstacles they've overcome, and what truly drives them.

Most candidates prepare to check boxes—experience, skills, qualifications. But when invited to tell their story, they can highlight their
personal journey, the obstacles they've overcome, and what truly drives them.

They can also use "Tell Me . . ." to guide the conversation in meaningful ways:

"Tell me what success looks like in this role."

"Tell me about the company's vision for the next five years."

"Tell me what you love most about working here."

By shifting from passive respondent to active participant, candidates move beyond the predictable Q&A format and create a conversation—one that feels natural, engaging, and memorable.

College Interviews: Uncovering Potential

For the Interviewer: Identify True Character

College admissions are flooded with high GPAs and leadership titles. But a great student isn't just defined by grades—they're shaped by resilience, curiosity, and personal growth.

⇒ Instead of asking, "What are your strengths?" say:

⇒ "Tell me about a time you were challenged."

⇒ "Tell me about a subject that changed the way you see the world."

⇒ "Tell me about a teacher or mentor who made a difference in your life."

This encourages students to share defining moments: the time they struggled with a subject but refused to give up, the community project they spearheaded, or the personal hardship that shaped their perspective. These stories reveal grit, determination, and emotional intelligence—traits that truly define a successful student.

Tell Me . . .

For the Interviewee: Show Your Curiosity and Ambition

Most students are eager to prove they're the right fit, but they can also use *Tell Me...* to learn more about the school and demonstrate intellectual curiosity.

They might inquire:

⇒ "Tell me about a student who thrived here and why."
⇒ "Tell me what sets this school apart academically."
⇒ "Tell me how students here engage with the local community."

By engaging their interviewer in a meaningful conversation, they not only learn valuable insights but also demonstrate confidence, initiative, and enthusiasm.

Exit Interviews: Finding the Real Reasons

Employees leaving a company often hold back, fearing they'll burn bridges. Asking, "Why are you leaving?" might only elicit a safe, diplomatic answer: "I got a great offer elsewhere." Instead, try:

⇒ "Tell me about your experience here."
⇒ "Tell me about a time when you felt truly valued."
⇒ "Tell me what we could have done differently."

This shifts the conversation from justification to reflection. Employees feel safer opening up about what worked, what didn't, and what could improve.

For the Interviewee: Leave a Lasting Impression

Departing employees can also use "Tell Me . . ." to maintain positive relationships and offer constructive feedback:

⇒ "Tell me how you see the company evolving over the next few years."
⇒ "Tell me what advice you'd give someone stepping into my role."

⇒ "Tell me what you've valued most about our time working together."

These questions help end the relationship on a positive, professional note, keeping the door open for future opportunities.

Performance Reviews: Encouraging Ownership
For the Interviewer: Foster Growth, Not Defensiveness

Performance reviews often feel like a list of critiques. Employees can become defensive, feeling scrutinized rather than supported.

Instead of saying, "Here's what you need to improve," try:

⇒ "Tell me about your biggest achievement this year."

⇒ "Tell me what challenges you've faced and how you tackled them."

⇒ "Tell me what support you need to grow." This encourages self-reflection and turns the review into a collaborative conversation rather than a one-sided evaluation.

For the Employee: Take Charge of Your Growth

Employees can use "Tell Me . . ." to proactively shape their career trajectory:

⇒ "Tell me what leadership opportunities you see for me."

⇒ "Tell me how I can contribute more to the company's success."

⇒ "Tell me about skills I should develop for my next step."

This transforms the review into a strategic discussion, showing initiative and a commitment to growth.

Conversations That Matter

In every interview setting, "Tell Me . . ." transforms the experience for both parties.

Tell Me . . .

For the *interviewer*, it shifts the focus from extracting information to understanding the person behind the answers. It reveals true motivations, builds trust, and leads to better decisions.

For the *interviewee*, it creates a space to be authentic, to share their story, and to engage in a conversation that feels meaningful rather than mechanical.

By incorporating "Tell Me . . ." on both sides of the conversation, interviews become more than assessments—they become opportunities for genuine connection, discovery, and insight.

So, in your next interview, whether you're asking the questions or answering them, resist the urge to stick to scripts. Instead, extend an invitation.

Simply say: "Tell Me . . ."

And watch the conversation—and its impact—transform.

Key Takeaways from Chapter 17

⇒ "Tell Me . . ." shifts the dynamic: Rather than asking direct questions that prompt rehearsed answers, try using "Tell Me . . ." to invite deeper reflection, personal stories, and authenticity, allowing for a more meaningful connection.
⇒ Job interviews become personal narratives.
⇒ College interviews uncover true potential.
⇒ Exit interviews yield real reasons for departure.
⇒ Performance reviews foster ownership.
⇒ Tell me YOUR key takeaway: _____

Action Item

Whether interviewer or interviewee, incorporate "Tell Me . . ." in your next interview. Replace conventional questions with "Tell me . . ." to invite deeper insights. For example, in a job interview, try, "Tell me what inspired you to pursue this career path?" This approach fosters more meaningful dialogue and uncovers qualities that go beyond surface-level responses.

"Ninety-nine percent of all failures come from people who have a habit of making excuses."

—George Washington Carver

Chapter 18

Tell Me About Accountability

In 1968, two psychologists, John Darley and Bibb Latané, conducted an experiment that would forever change how we think about human behavior in group settings.[21] Their study, inspired by the murder of Kitty Genovese, examined why individuals fail to act in emergencies when surrounded by others. What they discovered was the *bystander effect*, a phenomenon where people assume someone else will step up, so they do nothing. This discovery was groundbreaking, but what it really underscored is a broader truth: In many situations, the presence of others diminishes personal responsibility.

This idea of diminished responsibility shows up in all sorts of settings—far beyond emergencies. Think about the corporate world, where projects go awry, deadlines slip, and the crucial task of holding people accountable can feel as difficult as steering a ship through fog. It's easy to assume someone else will take charge, that the system will right itself, or that things will get better without intervention. But they don't. The problem deepens. And just like with the bystander effect, the larger the organization, the easier it is for accountability to slip through the cracks.

Tell Me . . .

The Problem with Accountability

Let's start with a basic truth: Holding people accountable is hard. It's one of those concepts that, on the surface, seems simple. If someone doesn't do what they were supposed to do, you call them out. If they succeed, you reward them. But in practice, accountability is more complex. It's less about tracking tasks and more about understanding motivations, expectations, and behavior—both individual and collective.

The reality is that accountability isn't about pointing fingers after the fact. It's about creating an environment where people are not only responsible for their actions but also feel a deep, intrinsic ownership over the outcomes of those actions. And this doesn't happen naturally in most corporate settings. Instead, there's a tendency for accountability to be diffuse, for responsibility to be spread so thin that no one feels truly accountable for anything.

This phenomenon manifests in all sorts of ways. Teams are given tasks, goals are set, and people agree to them. But then something happens. The deadline slips. The project hits a snag. Maybe the client gets frustrated. And slowly, the energy behind the initiative begins to drain away. What happens next? That's when the *bystander effect* kicks in. The team hopes someone else will take care of it, that the problem will resolve itself, that maybe the client won't notice.

But accountability doesn't work that way. When everyone assumes that someone else will step up, no one does.

Sarah's Story

Take the case of Sarah. She was a rising star at a consulting firm—a quick thinker, sharp communicator, and a favorite among clients. One of those clients was a major retail brand that had been loyal to Sarah's firm for several years. They relied on Sarah and her team to develop and execute marketing strategies for their product launches, and the relationship had always been strong.

But this time, things were different. The client had launched a new line of products, and Sarah's team was tasked with creating the campaign to support it. The timeline was tight, but nothing they hadn't handled before. Sarah, with her trademark confidence, promised the client they'd deliver.

Then, the first deadline was missed.

It wasn't a huge deal—Sarah reassured her team and the client that it was just a small hiccup, something they could recover from. But then the second deadline slipped. And then a third. The team was behind schedule, but instead of facing the issue, they continued to work in crisis mode, hoping that if they just pushed a little harder, they'd catch up.

At the same time, Sarah stopped responding to the client's increasingly frustrated emails. It wasn't that she didn't want to; it was that she didn't know what to say. Every time she sat down to reply, she felt paralyzed by the fear of admitting that things weren't going well. So she didn't.

The client, feeling ignored and anxious about the upcoming launch, finally requested a meeting. Sitting across the table from the client, Sarah stumbled through a series of vague reassurances. "We're almost there," she said. "We're just ironing out the last few details." The client was not convinced. In fact, they were on the verge of pulling the account entirely.

Sarah's failure wasn't just about missed deadlines or poor communication. It was a failure of accountability. From the moment things started to go wrong, she avoided taking ownership of the problem. She didn't address the issues with her team, hoping instead that they would fix themselves. She didn't confront the client with the reality of the delays, assuming they would understand if she stayed quiet long enough. But the reality is that accountability doesn't work that way. The more Sarah avoided the problem, the bigger it became, until it nearly cost her the entire relationship with one of the firm's most important clients.

Tell Me . . .

Apply the "Tell Me . . ." Principle

So what could Sarah have done differently? What can any of us do when faced with a similar situation?

The answer, surprisingly, is simple. It comes down to two words: "Tell me..."

Imagine if, early in the process, Sarah had approached her team and said, "Tell me what's going on." Not in an accusatory way, not as a demand for excuses, but as an invitation to reflect on the situation. It's a question that puts the responsibility back on the person you're asking. "Tell Me . . ." is open-ended, it's neutral, and it encourages the other person to articulate the problem in their own words. It shifts the conversation from "Why haven't you done this yet?" to "Let's figure out what's going wrong and how we can fix it."

"Tell Me . . ." also works on the client side. Imagine if, instead of waiting for the situation to escalate, Sarah had reached out to her client and said, "Tell me how you're feeling about the project so far." That one question could have opened up a dialogue, allowed the client to express their concerns, and given Sarah a chance to reset expectations. The simple act of asking a question could have shifted the dynamic from one of frustration to one of collaboration.

In both cases, the phrase "Tell me . . ." does something powerful: It creates accountability without confrontation. It invites ownership. Instead of Sarah telling her team what they were doing wrong or her client what they should expect, "Tell me . . ." asks for an explanation. And in doing so, it makes the other person reflect on their own role in the situation. It's a nudge, not a demand. And that's the key to real accountability—it's not about punishment; it's about ownership.

The Accountability Disconnect

What Sarah's story illustrates is something that happens all too often in corporate settings. People avoid accountability because they're afraid of the consequences. They worry about what will happen if they admit something has gone wrong. But the irony is, the longer they avoid it, the worse the consequences become. Accountability, when embraced early, can save relationships, projects, and even entire businesses. But when it's delayed, it compounds problems.

There's a cognitive bias at play here. Psychologists call it *loss aversion*—the idea that we fear losing something more than we value gaining something. In Sarah's case, she feared losing the client so much that she avoided confronting the problem head-on, thinking that by doing so, she might somehow salvage the relationship. But that fear of loss blinded her to the reality that the only way to save the relationship was to take ownership of the problem early.

"Tell me..." counteracts loss aversion because it reframes accountability as a conversation, not a confrontation. It takes the fear out of the equation and replaces it with curiosity. When we say "Tell me...," we're not looking for someone to blame. We're looking for a solution.

Be Comfortable Making Them Uncomfortable

Anisa, a top-tier executive at a major luxury hotel chain, was at her wit's end. One of her direct reports, Gunther, was perpetually late—for meetings, appointments, and even his own shifts. His chronic tardiness wasn't just an annoyance; it was a drain on team morale and productivity. His colleagues had to pick up the slack in his absence, and his lack of communication—no calls or messages to explain his lateness—made matters worse.

Tell Me . . .

When Anisa confronted Gunther about his behavior, the responses were always the same: a lame excuse or no excuse at all. Her reminders about the importance of punctuality seemed to fall on deaf ears. It was clear there was no accountability for his behavior, and Anisa, a consummate professional, was at a loss for how to handle it effectively.

During one of our coaching sessions, Anisa shared her frustration. I suggested a new approach, one that would subtly but powerfully shift the dynamic. "Anisa," I said, "the next time Gunther is late, invite him to your office. Have him sit down, and then calmly say, 'Gunther, tell me why you were late for the meeting today.' After he gives his excuse, follow up with, 'Tell me what measures you will take to ensure this doesn't happen again.' Make him articulate his plan for improvement. Make him uncomfortable, and he won't enjoy this process, and that's the point."

Anisa was skeptical but willing to try. The very next week, Gunther arrived late for a departmental meeting. True to plan, Anisa called him into her office afterward. As instructed, she asked, "Gunther, tell me why you were late for the meeting today." He fumbled for an excuse. She nodded and then continued, "Tell me what measures you will take to ensure this doesn't happen again." Gunther hesitated, clearly uncomfortable.

The next time Gunther was late, Anisa repeated the process. Each time, he squirmed a little more in his seat, struggling to answer her pointed questions. It wasn't long before Gunther had an epiphany: These were not conversations he wanted to keep having.

Within a few weeks, his tardiness stopped altogether. He began showing up on time, every time. The change was not only noticed but appreciated by his team, who no longer had to compensate for his absences. Anisa felt a sense of triumph—not just because Gunther had turned over a new leaf, but because she had effectively held him accountable in a way that was firm yet constructive. In fact, this was the foundation for every accountability conversation she had with any of her employees.

This simple strategy—starting with "Tell me . . ."—had unlocked a solution Anisa hadn't thought possible. It wasn't just about enforcing rules; it was about giving Gunther the opportunity to reflect, take ownership, and change. And that is the essence of true accountability.

Building a Culture of Accountability

Creating a culture of accountability in any organization is about more than just making sure tasks get done. It's about creating a space where people feel empowered to own their work, to be transparent about their challenges, and to engage in honest conversations about what's going well—and what's not.

The next time you're faced with a situation where accountability is slipping, resist the urge to assign blame. Instead, say, "Tell me . . ." Say it early, say it often, and say it without judgment. You'll be surprised how quickly it changes the dynamic. Because accountability, at its core, is about creating a culture where people feel responsible for the outcomes of their actions—and where they understand that they'll be asked to explain not just what went wrong, but how they're going to fix it.

In the end, accountability is less about assigning responsibility and more about inviting ownership.

And it all starts with a simple phrase: "Tell me . . ."

Key Takeaways from Chapter 18

⇒ Just like the bystander effect, accountability often diminishes in group settings where individuals assume someone else will act.
⇒ True accountability is about creating an environment where individuals feel ownership over their actions and outcomes, rather than pointing fingers after the fact.
⇒ Using the phrase "Tell me..." shifts the conversation from confrontation to collaboration, encouraging reflection and personal ownership without blame.
⇒ Fear of losing something (like a client) can cause people to avoid confronting problems.
⇒ Effective accountability is about fostering transparency, empowering individuals to take responsibility for their actions, and creating a culture of continuous improvement.
⇒ Tell me YOUR key takeaway:

_____

Action Item

Implement "Tell Me..." in accountability conversations. The next time accountability is slipping, instead of assigning blame, use "Tell me..." directives such as "Tell me why the report wasn't delivered at the scheduled time" or "Tell me how you're feeling about this situation." This encourages reflection and ownership, creating a productive dialogue that leads to solutions and reinforces accountability.

"In order for collaboration to take place, managers must give up their silos and their perceptions of power.

—*Jane Ripley*

Chapter 19

Silos Are for Grains, not Brains

Breaking Down the Silos

In the modern workplace, silos are a common but often detrimental phenomenon. They are the invisible barriers that form between departments, teams, and even individuals within an organization, leading to a lack of communication, collaboration, and a shared vision. Isolationism becomes the norm. When silos form, teams operate in isolation, unaware of how their actions negatively impact other teams or how they could work together toward their common goal. Breaking down these silos is crucial for fostering a culture of cooperation and innovation. This chapter will explore how a simple phrase, "Tell me . . . ," can bridge these gaps and lead to productive collaborations, illustrated by an anecdotal story of two coworkers.

The Story of Mark and Lisa

Mark was a senior engineer at TechSolutions, a mid-sized tech company known for its innovative products. Mark was brilliant at what he did but was also known for working in isolation. His desk, tucked away in a corner, was

Tell Me . . .

piled high with blueprints and prototypes. He rarely interacted with colleagues outside of his immediate team and was often perceived as unapproachable.

On the other hand, Lisa was a dynamic marketing manager who had recently joined TechSolutions. She was outgoing and always eager to share ideas and collaborate with others. However, she quickly became aware of a lack of communication between the engineering and marketing departments, which was affecting the company's ability to launch new products effectively and on time.

One day while visiting the engineering floor, Lisa stumbled upon a project Mark was working on. She was intrigued by the prototype she saw but hesitated to approach Mark, knowing his reputation. However, she decided to take a chance and walked up to him.

"Hi, Mark. I'm Lisa from marketing. I couldn't help but notice the prototype on your desk. It looks fascinating. Could you tell me more about it?" Lisa asked with a warm smile.

Mark looked up, surprised. He wasn't used to people from other departments showing interest in his work. "Uh, sure," he replied, unsure of what to expect. "This is a new product we're developing. It's still in the early stages."

Lisa listened intently as Mark explained the concept behind the prototype. She asked questions, not just out of curiosity but to understand the technical aspects better. As Mark explained, he began to realize that Lisa's questions were not just about the product but about how it could be positioned in the market, what problems it could solve for customers, and how it could align with the company's overall strategy.

"Tell Me . . ." Changes Things

The simple phrase "Tell me . . ." had opened a door that had been shut for too long. Lisa's genuine interest and willingness to listen without judgment made Mark feel valued and understood. It was the beginning of a conversation that would change the dynamic between the two departments.

Over the next few weeks, Lisa and Mark started meeting regularly. Lisa would ask Mark to tell her about his latest projects, and in return, she would share insights from the market, customer feedback, and potential marketing strategies. This exchange of information began to break down the silos between engineering and marketing.

One day, during one of their meetings, Mark mentioned a challenge he was facing with the prototype. "We're having trouble finding the right materials that are both cost-effective and durable," he explained.

"Tell me more about the requirements," Lisa responded. As Mark detailed the specifications, Lisa had an idea. "I recently attended a trade show where I met a supplier who specializes in innovative materials. I think they might have something that fits your needs. How about I set up a meeting with them?"

Mark was initially skeptical but agreed to give it a try. The meeting with the supplier was a success, and they found a material that not only met the technical requirements but was also cost-effective. This breakthrough accelerated the development of the product.

Building a Collaborative Culture

The collaboration between Mark and Lisa did not go unnoticed. Other employees began to see the benefits of breaking down silos and started adopting the "Tell Me . . ." approach. It became a part of the company's culture to seek out colleagues from different departments and genuinely listen to their perspectives and challenges.

Tell Me . . .

The leadership team at TechSolutions recognized the positive impact of this cultural shift. They started encouraging cross-departmental projects and initiatives. Regular inter-departmental meetings were held where employees could share updates, discuss challenges, and brainstorm solutions together. The phrase "Tell Me . . ." became a catalyst for these conversations, fostering an environment of openness and collaboration.

One notable project that emerged from this new culture was the development of a customer feedback loop. The marketing team, led by Lisa, worked closely with the engineering and customer support teams to create a system where customer feedback was collected, analyzed, and quickly integrated into product development. This not only improved the products but also increased customer satisfaction and loyalty.

A Ripple Effect

The impact of breaking down silos extended beyond internal operations. TechSolutions began to see improved market performance, faster product development cycles, and increased employee satisfaction. The company's reputation as an innovative and collaborative workplace attracted top talent, further fueling its growth.

Mark and Lisa's story became a cornerstone of the company's success narrative. It was frequently shared in company meetings and onboarding sessions as an example of how a simple act of asking "Tell Me . . ." can lead to significant positive changes.

One day, during a company-wide town hall, the CEO addressed the employees. "We have always been a company that values innovation, but innovation cannot thrive in isolation. It's the collaboration, the sharing of ideas, and the willingness to listen to each other that drives us forward. Remember the power of 'Tell me . . .' It's more than just a phrase; it's a mindset that can break down barriers and open up endless possibilities."

Silos Are for Grains, not Brains

Silos are designed for storing grain, not for storing our brains. Operating in a silo deprives others of our talents and insights, limiting both individual and organizational growth. The story of Mark and Lisa at TechSolutions illustrates how a simple phrase like "Tell Me . . ." can initiate meaningful conversations, foster collaboration, and lead to remarkable outcomes.

In professional, social, and family conversations, "Tell Me . . ." can be a powerful tool to bridge gaps, understand different perspectives, and build stronger relationships. It encourages openness, curiosity, and empathy, which are crucial for effective communication and collaboration.

As you navigate your own conversations, whether at work, at home, or in social settings, remember the impact of asking someone to tell you their story, their ideas, or their challenges. You might be surprised at how much you can learn and how much you can achieve together.

Key Takeaways from Chapter 19

⇒ Silos form when departments or individuals operate in isolation, which leads to a lack of communication and hampers innovation.
⇒ Collaboration and innovation die in silence.
⇒ Isolation can be extremely dangerous and can lead to decreased employee engagement and lower productivity.
⇒ Silos limit individual and organizational growth.
⇒ Tell me YOUR key takeaway:

_____

Action Item

Begin using the phrase "Tell me . . ." in your daily interactions with colleagues, clients, friend, and family members to break down barriers and foster collaboration. Asking "Tell me more about that" or "Tell me how you're approaching this" will create opportunities for meaningful conversations and help build a more connected, innovative work, social, and family environment.

"Good conversation is not only satisfying, It's the first step toward changing the world."

—*Jay Walljasper*

Chapter 20

Ripple, Resonate, Reshape

There's a principle that's often overlooked when we think about conversations: There are no neutral encounters. Every interaction we have, every word we choose, every gesture we make—it either lifts someone up or pushes them down. There is no middle ground.

This might sound extreme but think about it. The way you engage with someone changes them, if only a little. A smile or a kind word can brighten someone's day, while an offhand remark or a dismissive tone can dampen their spirit. The impact may be small, or it may be significant, but it's there. And that's the truth we often fail to recognize: Our words and actions create ripples that resonate far beyond the moment, reshaping everyone they encounter.

The Unseen Ripples of Our Words

Consider this: Every conversation you have is a moment of influence. Whether it's a brief exchange at the coffee shop or a deep discussion with a close friend, you are constantly shaping the experience of the person in front of you. When you say to someone, "Tell me more," you're not just inviting them to speak—you're giving them a moment to feel valued, to feel heard. And that changes them.

But it doesn't stop there. The person you lift up will carry that feeling forward into their next interaction. The positivity you create has a way of spreading, often to people you'll never meet. On the other hand, if your words or actions push someone down, the effects of that negativity ripple outward too, shaping their interactions in ways that can dampen the energy of everyone they touch.

This is the power of conversation—it's a constant cycle of influence, whether we realize it or not. There is no neutral.

Conversations That Change Worlds

Let me take you back to a seemingly simple moment. It's a quiet morning at a park bench, and a woman sits, lost in thought, her shoulders weighed down by an unseen burden. A stranger walking by notices her somber expression and pauses. With a gentle smile, he says, "Tell me what's on your mind."

Surprised, but moved by the sincerity in his voice, the woman hesitates, then begins to speak. She shares that she's an artist, struggling with self-doubt, wondering if her work matters to anyone. The stranger listens attentively, nodding thoughtfully, and when she finishes, he says, "Your work matters because *you* matter. Don't stop creating—you never know who might need to see the world through your eyes."

The conversation, though brief, is transformative. The woman feels seen, valued, and uplifted at a moment when she needed it most. As she leaves the park, a spark of confidence reignites within her. She smiles at the cashier at a nearby café, compliments the barista on their latte art, and takes the time to encourage a fellow artist online.

Ripple, Resonate, Reshape

The ripple effect grows and resonates with each person she encounters. Her warmth inspires the café staff to be extra kind to their next customers. Her online encouragement gives another struggling artist the motivation to keep going. Every person she touches carries forward her renewed positivity, influencing countless others. She has reshaped her world and the world of others.

And yet, none of this would have happened without those two simple words: "Tell me . . ." In that moment, the stranger's interest and kindness created a ripple of connection and hope, spreading far beyond what he could have imagined.

This is the power of intentional words and actions. A single moment of care can uplift someone at a critical juncture, changing not just their day but the days of everyone they touch.

And the reverse is true. An unkind word, a dismissive gesture—these, too, have a lasting impact. When we push someone down, we create ripples of negativity that echo outward, coloring the next conversation, the next interaction, the next decision. The world is reshaped in subtle ways that add up over time.

In this way, no encounter is insignificant. No conversation is without consequence.

The Myth of Neutrality

We like to believe that most of our conversations are neutral. That there's a middle ground, where we neither help nor harm. But neutrality is an illusion. When we choose to disengage, to remain indifferent, or to gloss over moments of real connection, we miss opportunities to lift others up. And that, in itself, is a loss.

Psychologists have studied the effects of emotional contagion—the idea that our emotions spread to those around us, even without words. Just think

Tell Me . . .

about a cheering crowd at a sporting event. It's impossible to passively sit in your seat when everyone is on their feet yelling with excitement when your team scores. Whether we realize it or not, our mood, our body language, our tone—all of it is communicating something. Even in silence, we are shaping the world around us. So, when you opt out of engaging fully with someone, you're not maintaining the status quo. You're contributing to a missed opportunity for connection. And in that void, negativity often finds room to grow.

Your Words, Your World

Imagine a world where every conversation, every interaction, was treated as an opportunity to lift someone up. What kind of world would that create? It wouldn't be perfect—there would still be missteps, misunderstandings, and conflict. But the ripples of positive engagement would spread. They would reshape how we relate to each other, how we see ourselves, and how we navigate the challenges of life.

The truth is, the way we speak to others is a reflection of how we view the world. If we approach conversations with curiosity and kindness, we begin to create a world that reflects those values. When we say to someone, "Tell me more," we're not just seeking information—we're saying, "You matter. Your thoughts matter. Your experience matters." In doing so, we begin to build a world where people feel seen, heard, and valued.

No Conversation Stands Alone

It's easy to think of conversations as discrete events—moments that begin and end within the span of minutes or hours. But in reality, no conversation stands alone. Every word, every gesture, every question you ask is part of a larger narrative. And that narrative continues to evolve long after the conversation is over.

Think of your words as stones dropped into a pond. Each word creates ripples, and those ripples spread out, touching everything in their path. You may never see where those ripples end, but they do end somewhere. And in their wake, they leave behind a world that is subtly changed by your presence.

The Responsibility of Engagement

At its core, recognizing that there are no neutral encounters is about taking responsibility for how we engage with others. It's about acknowledging that we are always having an impact—whether positive or negative. And it's about making the conscious choice to bring people up rather than push them down.

In the end, this is what meaningful conversation is all about. It's not just about exchanging information; it's about creating positive ripples in the lives of others. It's about recognizing the power you have to reshape the world around you—one interaction at a time.

So, as you move forward, ask yourself: What kind of ripples do you want to create? When you say to someone, "Tell Me . . . ," what kind of impact are you hoping to have? Because in every encounter, you are shaping not just their world, but your world, and ultimately, our world.

And there's nothing neutral about that.

Tell Me . . .

Key Takeaways from Chapter 20

Tell me YOUR key takeaway (it's really the most important one relative to this chapter):

_____

_____

_____

_____

_____

_____

Action Item

Remember, you have the power to make a lasting impact. Every word and action you take creates ripples that resonate with those around you, reshaping their world, your world, and even our world. Start today by creating those ripples with the simple phrase, "Tell me . . ." It's a small step that can spark meaningful change and leave a profound mark on the people you interact with.

The Beginning of the Beginning

Your New Story Begins

As you turn the last page and close this book, I want you to reflect on the simple yet profound moment that inspired it all. When James Earl Jones looked at his adoring fan and said, "Tell me your name," he wasn't merely asking a question—he was offering the gift of recognition, of making someone feel seen and valued. That moment is a reminder of the immense power of connection, a power that now lies in your hands.

The phrase "Tell me . . ." is your tool—a versatile and transformative key to deeper, more meaningful relationships. Whether in professional settings, at social gatherings, or in the quiet moments with loved ones, it can bridge gaps, build trust, and spark genuine conversations. But let me be clear: Simply reading this book won't change you. True transformation requires *intentionality*.

If you want to unlock the full potential of "Tell me . . . ," you must put it into practice. Use it in the workplace to engage your colleagues and clients. Let it guide your conversations at social events to move beyond small talk. In your personal life, lean on it to strengthen the bonds that matter most. Every time you choose to say, "Tell me . . . ," you take a step toward becoming someone who connects, understands, and inspires.

It won't always be easy, and not every interaction will unfold as planned. That's part of the process. Each conversation, whether smooth or challenging, will help you grow. Over time, you'll sharpen your skills, develop greater empathy, and discover the richness that comes from truly listening.

Tell Me . . .

And now, I'd love to hear from you. *Tell me* how this book has impacted the way you approach conversations in your professional, social, and family life. Has it given you more confidence in starting meaningful discussions? Helped you build stronger relationships? Led to a breakthrough moment? Please take a moment to share a positive experience where something you learned in this book made a real difference. Your story could be highlighted in my follow-up book showing the impact of *Tell Me . . .* "on the lives of some of the readers. Click the link or scan the QR code to provide your feedback—I truly value your insights.

Remember, "Tell me . . ." is more than a phrase—it's an invitation, a bridge, and a catalyst for transformation. Use it *boldly* and *intentionally*. Make every conversation count. The stories are waiting. Are you ready to listen? Are you ready to share?

With gratitude and encouragement,

Fred

Use this QR code to provide your feedback

https://bit.ly/3Gufv1j

Acknowledgments

Tell Me... would not have been possible without the love, friendship, and support of so many who encouraged and believed in me and the message this book is meant to deliver.

To you, the reader—thank you. You've taken a chance on this book and, in doing so, on me as a first-time author. That means more than I can express. Writing "Tell Me..." has been a journey fueled by curiosity, experience, and a deep belief in the power of meaningful conversations. But a book is only as valuable as the impact it has on those who read it.

I hope these pages inspire you to step into conversations with greater confidence, to listen with intention, and to embrace the stories waiting to be shared. If this book has helped you in any way, then it has done its job.

To my wife, Patricia—my rock, my inspiration, and my greatest supporter: Through every pursuit in my life, both brilliant and not-so-brilliant, you have stood by me with unwavering belief and encouragement. For forty years of love, patience, and partnership, I am endlessly grateful.

To my daughters, Simone and Sara; their husbands, Chris and Dan; and my grandchildren, Jolie, Missy, Joe, Ella, and Emilio: You are my greatest legacy. Your curiosity, kindness, and spirit ensure that the essence of meaningful conversation lives on in our family for generations to come.

To Marvin LeBlanc, author of *Come Hell or High Water*, whose mentorship and relentless prodding pushed me to complete this book—even when

Tell Me . . .

I thought I couldn't: Your friendship and belief in me have meant more than words can express.

To Jeff Martin, author of *Business Mulligan*, the first to recognize that this book was inside me, waiting to be written: Your encouragement and friendship set this journey in motion, and for that, I am forever grateful. You have always been in the *Fred business!*

To my father, Emile, his brothers Sammie and Edmund, and his sister, Yvonne—masters of conversation and connection: Through their stories, wisdom, and example, I learned that conversation is the foundation of all great relationships. Their voices echo throughout these pages.

To my mother, Marguerite—Her letters, so rich in depth and grace, reflected the heart that always beat in rhythm with mine. She was my fiercest champion, my unwavering source of encouragement, and the first to believe in every dream I dared to chase. The warmth of her love still burns within me, lighting my path every day.

To my brother, E.A., who was blessed beyond measure with the "talk-your-ear-off" gift of gab. No one I have ever known enjoyed engaging in conversation and storytelling more than he did—not even close. His ability to captivate, connect, and entertain through words was a gift to all who had the pleasure of knowing him. His spirit lives on in every meaningful conversation, every shared story, and in the very essence of this book.

To Sister Mary Isabel of the Sisters of the Most Holy Sacrament Order, my kindergarten and first-grade teacher, who gave me the gift of reading and writing: Without that foundation, this book—and so much more—would never have been possible.

Notes

To the legendary actor, James Earl Jones, whose simple yet powerful words, "Tell me your name," resonated with me over the decades and provided the insight and inspiration for this book: His ability to transform words into connection was a masterclass in the power of conversation.

To the countless friends, colleagues, and relatives who took the time to read the manuscript and offer encouragement: Your feedback, insights, and support made this journey even more meaningful.

Notes

1. *Cambridge Dictionary* (2025), under "conversation."
2. "'It Could Have Been an Email' Almost Half of Youn Professionals View Work Calls and Meetings as Inefficient," Robert Walters, May 15, 2024, https://bit.ly/41mJlwk.
3. Simon Sinek, *Start with Why: How Great Leaders Inspire Everyone to Take Action* (Penguin Books, 2009), 38–51.
4. Jay L. Hoecker, MD, "Infant and Toddler Health," Healthy Lifestyle, Mayo Clinic, March 4, 2023, https://bit.ly/415IVcp.
5. Jonathan Haidt, The Anxious Generation: How the Great Rewiring of Childhood Is Causing an Epidemic of Mental Illness (Penguin, 2024).
6. "Impostor Syndrome," *Psychology Today*, accessed December 16, 2024, https://bit.ly/417w4Xv.
7. Aditi Subramaniam, PhD, "All Eyes on Us: The Spotlight Effect," *Psychology Today*, June 20, 2022, https://bit.ly/4kOZYVR.
8. Interview with J. K. Rowling, The Rowling Library, originally aired on ITN, October 8, 1998, https://bit.ly/3EFIVZp.
9. Dale Carnegie Training, *Make Yourself Unforgettable: How to Become the Person Everyone Remembers and No One Can Resist* (Simon & Schuster, 2011), 30.
10. R. I. M. Dunbar, "The Social Brain Hypothesis and Its Implications for Social Evolution," *Annals of Human Biology*, 36, no. 5 (September–October 2009): 562–572, https://bit.ly/41mwZEA.
11. Jessica R. Andrews-Hanna, "The Brain's Default Network and Its Adaptive Role in Internal Mentation," *Neuroscientist*, 18, no. 3 (June 15, 2011): 251–270, https://bit.ly/4k1kjKL.

12. Livia Tomova, et al., "Acute Social Isolation Evokes Midbrain Craving Responses Similar to Hunger," *Nature Neuroscience*, 23, no. 12 (December 23, 2020): 1597–1605, https://bit.ly/4gKtbl1.
13. Goran Simić, et al., "Understanding Emotions: Origins and Roles of the Amygdala," *Biomolecules*, 11, no. 6 (May 31, 2021): 823, https://bit.ly/4i5rgsg.
14. Matt Johnson, PhD, "How Two Brains Synchronize in Conversation," *Psychology Today*, updated December 8, 2024, https://shorturl.at/myHhz.
15. Nicklas Balboa and Richard D. Glaser, PhD, "The Neuroscience of Conversation," *Psychology Today*, May 16, 2019, https://shorturl.at/YnMHE.
16. "Ten Minutes of Talking Has a Mental Payoff," Michigan News, University of Michigan, October 29, 2007, https://shorturl.at/T8qRz.
17. Joe Navarro, *What Every Body Is Saying: An Ex-FBI Agent's Guide to Speed-Reading People,* with Marvin Karlins, PhD (Harper Collins, 2008).
18. Rindy C. Anderson, et al., "Vocal Fry May Undermine the Success of Young Women in the Labor Market," *PLoS ONE*, 9, no. 5 (May 28, 2014), https://shorturl.at/fyczH.
19. Ariel Craine, "Fifteen Common English Filler Words You Should Know," Speechling.com, April 2, 2021, https://shorturl.at/fghSj.
20. Albert Mehrabian, *Silent Messages* (Wadsworth Publishing Company, 1971).
21. Ruud Hortensius and Beatrice de Gelder, "From Empathy to Apathy: The Bystander Effect Revisited," *Current Directions in Psychological Science*, 27, no. 4 August 1, 2018): 249–256, https://shorturl.at/nT4mm.

A Library of Conversations

Books that will give you something to talk about

Act Natural: How to Speak to Any Audience, Ken Howard
Atomic Habits: An Easy and Proven Way to Build Good Habits and Break Bad Ones, James Clear
Beyond Resilience, Dan Diamond
Breaking the Code, Rusty Gaillard
Developing the Leader Within You, John C. Maxwell
Do It! Speaking: 77 Instant-Action Ideas to Market, Monetize, and Maximize Your Expertise, David Newman
Drive: The Surprising Truth About What Motivates Us, Daniel Pink
Four Seasons: The Story of a Business Philosophy, Isadore Sharp
Helping Teens with Stress, Anxiety, and Depression, Roy Petitfils
How to Talk So People Will Listen, Steve Brown
How to Win Friends and Influence People, Dale Carnegie
Human-Centered Communication, Ethan Beute and Stephen Pacinelli
Leaders Eat Last, Simon Sinek
Leadership and Self-Deception, The Arbinger Institute
Made to Stick, Chip Heath and Dan Heath
Meet Them Where They Are, Jen Croneberger
No Excuses!, Brian Tracy
Outliers, Malcolm Gladwell
Powered by Storytelling, Murray Nossel, PhD

Tell Me . . .

Red Light Green Light: How Top Leaders Present with Polish, Get Buy-in, and Become More Influential, Cindy Skalicky
Smash the Silos, Kiki Orski
Start with Why, Simon Sinek
Sticking Points: How to Get Five Generations Working Together in the Twelve Places They Come Apart, Haydn Shaw
The Anxious Generation, Jonathan Haidt
The 5 Second Rule, Mel Robbins
The Four Agreements, Don Miguel Ruiz
The Greatest Salesman in the World, Og Mandino
The Icarus Deception, Seth Godin
The Magic of Thinking Big, David J. Schwartz, Ph.D.
The Power of Habit: Why We Do What We Do in Life and Business, Charles Duhigg
The Power of Positive Thinking, Norman Vincent Peale
The Presentation Secrets of Steve Jobs, Carmine Gallo
The 7 Habits of Highly Effective People, Stephen R. Covey
The Slight Edge, Jeff Olson
The 12 Week Year, Brian P. Moran and Michael Lennington
Think and Grow Rich, Napoleon Hill
Thinking for a Change, John C. Maxwell
This Was Not in the Brochure: Lessons from Work, Ministry, and Life Mike Patin
What Got You Here Won't Get You There, Marshall Goldsmith
What Every Body Is Saying, Joe Navarro
Woo, Wow, and Win, Thomas A. Stewart and Patricia O'Connell

About The Author

Fred Reggie is an executive coach, international speaker, and respected authority on leadership, communication, service culture development, and nonprofit governance. He has successfully guided Fortune 500 executives, service-driven companies, and nonprofit leaders and their teams in building meaningful connections, strengthening organizational culture, and driving sustainable excellence.

An engaging storyteller and passionate communicator, Fred delivers practical tools to navigate conversations with confidence and authenticity. As an Eagle Scout and former national board member of St. Jude Children's Research Hospital, he exemplifies his belief in the power of service, leadership, and relationships.

In *Tell Me...*, Fred shares proven strategies to help readers build connections and create lasting impact in both their personal and professional lives.

Contact Fred . . .

. . . to inquire about:

⇒ Speaking engagements
⇒ Executive Coaching
⇒ Bulk book purchase discounts for your team

Scan the QR Code to schedule a call with Fred

www.ingramcontent.com/pod-product-compliance
Lightning Source LLC
Chambersburg PA
CBHW020654060526
44119CB00069B/56